MORTON GROVE PUBLIC LIBRARY
P9-DHL-841

# POWERHOUSE PLANTS

Morton Grove Public Library
6140 Lincoln Avenue
Morton Grove, IL 60053
847-965-4220

# POWERHOUSE
## PLANTS

### 510 TOP PERFORMERS
### FOR MULTI-SEASON BEAUTY

**GRAHAM RICE**
**photography by**
**judywhite and Graham Rice**

TIMBER PRESS
Portland · London

# Contents

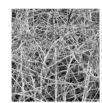

# Introduction

Most gardeners hoping to create attractive gardens think first of flowers. But plants have so many other appealing features, beauties that add color and shape and texture, bringing life to our lives and our gardens. Every aspect of a plant, from its emerging spring shoots to its lofty maturity, has the potential to inspire interest and admiration—or just to bring us pure color.

But why stop at plants that do just one thing, have just one appeal? Why not choose powerhouse plants that have more than one season of interest? These are plants that offer two or more entirely different features so that, at different times of the year, different displays are produced at the same place in the garden—from just one plant.

Such multi-talented plants are especially valuable in small yards where every inch is precious. What better way to make the most of a limited space than to create different displays at various times—in different seasons, or perhaps just a few weeks apart—from just one plant? In larger spaces, plants with more than one season of interest bring an enhanced richness, a new diversity, an intensity missing in normal plantings. Walking through your garden to admire your plants will take at least twice as long! Finally, plants that shine at more than one season allow different plant combinations to be created with neighboring plants at different times. Another stretch for your imagination, true, but so rewarding.

And never think that plants with multi-season appeal are rare or obscure or are only discovered by a diligent search of the country's specialist nurseries. Many will be found in your local nursery or garden center. You need only to look. Once the idea is implanted in your mind, you'll notice these powerhouse plants. And

◀ The pale dusty flowerheads of *Pennisetum alopecuroides* are set against bright summer foliage—then in fall, the whole plant has an exciting new look.

when looking at a plant in flower at the nursery, you'll find yourself asking: "What else does it do?"

All year, and especially through the winter, there are trees and large shrubs whose colorful or beautifully patterned bark brings as much brightness and satisfying structure and design as any flowers. Later, some will bring us vivid flowers or colorful fruits and especially fall color—but some will not.

On a smaller scale there are shrubs whose twigs are so brilliantly colored that they outshine the early bulbs planted below them. For some, their winter stem color is the beginning and end of their contribution to the garden, and for the rest of the year their primary function is to host to a viticella clematis. But some continue into spring with flowers, or take us through the summer with variegated foliage; some will develop fruits, and a few offer leaves that will turn colorful autumnal shades. The choice of variety is crucial.

As spring greets us with its surge of new growth, the bright emergence of new shoots on trees and shrubs and the fresh new growth on perennials as their shoots shoulder aside our mulch is an effect not always appreciated. And the fact is that most gardeners do not grow plants for this feature—they grow them for whatever comes next. But choose well, and a whole new phase of spring appeal becomes the opening act to summer flowers or a long season of attractive foliage.

▶ The amber tones of the new spring shoots on *Physocarpus opulifolius* 'Coppertina' ('Mindia') soon give way to copper and greenish tones, then mature to reddish bronze. In late autumn the leaves develop a sharper, almost translucent coloring, which looks well with maples.

Reflecting upon how plants carry themselves through the winter is not something that occupies most gardeners for a great deal of time. Perhaps we should think about it, though, for there are perennials, biennials, and annuals whose overwintering state is a bold and attractive rosette of ground-hugging wintergreen foliage which, later in spring or summer, is transformed into a very different floral display. But when so much around them is simply bare, their presence is invaluable—even if siting them so we can admire both their rosettes and what may be a similarly bold floral presence is challenging.

Foliage as a crucial element of the garden picture is something that has become important to gardeners only in relatively recent horticultural times. But whether it be bold, variegated, lacy, bronzed, fingered, golden, strident, purple . . . As has so often been said, not least by me over the years, foliage is around for so much longer than fleeting flowers—it deserves our respect.

In its vast variety, good foliage is indispensable in any garden. In shape, texture, color, and pattern, it is always with us. But while plants which do no more than show off their leaves are indispensable, what if they did more? What if they also produced flowers, or their winter bark was exceptionally colorful or prettily textured? What if, in the fall, or all through the seasons they are present, their foliage was

◀ The daintily marbled foliage of *Ampelopsis brevipedunculata* var. *maximowiczii* 'Elegans' is followed by attractive blue berries. In the autumn, the white-marbled foliage develops these buttery tones, transforming the plant into a cloud of yellow. In some areas, the plant becomes invasive as the birds distribute the berries.

▶ Long before the purplish red flowers of *Paeonia mascula* open, the bold red new growth surges dramatically through scattered *Anemone blanda*.

▶ As this prolific purple epimedium, 'Eco Violet Princess', is at its peak, the new purple spear of a dark form of *Arisaema triphyllum* emerges. The fresh red-edged foliage of 'Eco Violet Princess' follows its flowers and expands alongside the emerging spathe of *Arisaema triphyllum*. As the foliage of 'Eco Violet Princess' matures to deep green, the tight cluster of red berries on *Arisaema triphyllum* shines against the dark background.

transformed into new colors? Choose well, and all this could be yours.

For as the days continue to shorten after summer, the leaves of many trees and shrubs, and a few perennials, take on classically autumnal hues. We depend on them as the summer falters and the year starts to fade away. But how very much better if they did more. If their spring growth unfurled in an intriguing manner . . . if they flowered in summer . . . if their fruits were colorful and attracted birds (or if we could eat the fruits ourselves). Fortunately there are plants exactly like this.

Of course, for most gardeners flowers are the priority. We grow food and we grow flowers. But what if all those plants that bloom so prolifically across the seasons and engulf us with such intoxicating fragrance, what if before and after their entrancing blooms, they were more than just lumps of green? Perhaps their flowers are followed by colorful berries, or their bright stems enliven the winter garden. Perhaps, if the right varieties are chosen, their new shoots will be brilliant red and erupt colorfully through spring anemones.

Come the fall, the spring and summer flowers of many plants are maturing into fruit. In some cases, these fruits may prove small, dry, unremarkable, and, from the gardener's point of view, pointless. But birds or other creatures will appreciate them and come to the garden to feed. Then there are the fat berries, in such a convention of shades—the challenge

is to choose neighboring plants that make good partners both at flowering time and again in fall.

So break down plants' appeals into their components. What are the individual elements, the specific qualities that plants bring to our gardens?

- Bark
- Winter stems
- Winter and spring foliage rosettes
- New spring shoots pushing through the soil
- Fresh, unfurling foliage
- Summer foliage
- Evergreen foliage
- Fall foliage color
- Flowers
- Fruits

Choose almost any two of these qualities, and varieties can be found that successfully combine then. These are the beautiful, hardworking plants we want in the garden.

And then there are more than that, features not in that universal list which are less tangible, perhaps, less universally appreciated, including fragrance, elegance of habit, and edible qualities. These will all surface as I discuss the merits of individual plants providing additional delight or satisfaction. For that is the essence of the unexpectedly wide selection of plants I include in this book: each brings together at least two—sometimes three or even four—individual features and shows them at different times of the year, or adds a sparkling new feature to continuing display.

Now, let's highlight a few of the most valuable combinations of attractions that characterize the very best garden plants.

## Spring flowers/fall fruits

In spring, much of the attraction of the more substantial plants along natural woodland edges and in the garden comes from the flowering of shrubs.

We see it in the British hedgerows, where sloe or blackthorn (*Prunus spinosa*) sets off the flowering season with its clouds of white to be followed later by sloes, the tart purple-blue fruits, which are favorites with birds and which flavor the traditional British country specialty, sloe gin. In our part of Pennsylvania, the American elderberry (*Sambucus canadensis*) is one of the first flowering shrubs we see along roadsides, and after gathering a few berries and sowing them, we now have them in the wild corners of our garden, the robins enjoying the blue-black fall berries after we and pollinating insects have enjoyed the May flowers.

On both sides of the Atlantic, in both gardens and natural areas, viburnums in their many forms are crucial, as are hollies and barberries and dogwoods, some with the additional contribution of evergreen foliage. Cotoneasters, roses . . . There is a wide choice of appealing combinations in flower and fruit color.

On a larger scale, crabapples and other trees also provide a classic flowers-then-fruit spectacle; and at the other end of the scale, actaeas, a few iris, peonies, and several members of the lily family offer a less conspicuous version of the same sequential pairing.

## Winter twigs/summer foliage

The main contribution of an invaluable group of dogwoods and willows is to enliven our winter garden with their bright bare twigs in red, orange, yellow, green, and even in black and in combinations of colors. They are especially delightful undercarpeted

▼ Choose thoughtfully, and you'll find a few select varieties of a plant have that vital second season of interest. This is *Alstroemeria* 'Princess Fabiana' ('Zaprifabi') before it flowers.

with dwarf early bulbs. But in summer they look—well, "unremarkable" would be a kind word. Or at least most of them do.

Others however, when the spring buds burst, reveal variegated or golden summer foliage that adds a whole new look right through into the fall. The trick, as is so often the case when you need something a little special, is to choose the right variety. This is also a case when the right pruning—simple, but necessary and at the right time—greatly enhances the display, emphasizing the natural color that these tough and dependable shrubs bring to the garden.

Why grow a plant that looks good

◀ The berries of deciduous American hollies, *Ilex verticillata* 'Winter Red' and 'Winter Gold', follow inconspicuous spring flowers. The pattern is matched in the British native evergreen holly, *I. aquifolium*.

▼ The British native *Prunus spinosa* has an unusual trio of features. First the flowers, then the fruits—and finally the winter treat, sloe gin.

for one season when you can choose a variety that looks good for two, three, or all four? Some dogwoods do just that, if they flower well and the flowers mature to colorful fruits.

## Winter and spring foliage rosettes/summer flowers

Many plants, especially biennials and winter annuals but also some perennials, overwinter in the form of a rosette of foliage. Then in spring the flowers erupt, often on tall stems.

▼ The colorful winter stems of this willow, *Salix alba* 'Britzensis', are followed not by variegated foliage but by yellow catkins.

Think dandelions—or, better still, meconopsis, love-in-a-mist, and verbascum.

So over the winter and into the early days of spring, the broad felted foliage of verbascums and some meconopsis, for example, may be the only feature in an otherwise inescapably empty border. The more robust but less dominating of spring bulbs, like chionodoxa and scilla, make ideal companions if the colors are chosen to relate to those of the rosettes. Interestingly, birds and certain species of bees line their nests with the down collected from verbascum leaves, so value to wildlife is another variation on our theme of the multiple beauties and uses of well-chosen plants.

Often plants that form rosettes need placing towards the back of the border, as the candelabric eruption of some of the major verbascums is just too imposing, not to say tall, for anywhere else. But their rosettes are usually bold enough to stand out, even when glimpsed at a distance.

Many Mediterranean annuals—cornflowers, poppies, chrysanthemums—start to grow from their germinating seeds in late summer or early fall, develop broad and often striking rosettes, and flower in late spring and early summer; this is their natural cycle: they behave as winter annuals. In gardens, we tend to sow in spring for summer flowers, and the display of both rosettes and flowers is often less impressive. However, if we replicate their natural cycle, we

◀ Rosettes of foliage are a valuable, but often forgotten, winter feature. The silvery foliage of *Meconopsis napaulensis* is followed by towers of pink or reddish flowers.

◀ The sensuously silver rosette of *Verbascum bombyciferum* 'Silver Lining', with *Euphorbia characias* in front, has gathered strength for its eruption of flower. As the silky winter foliage fades, the verbascum's candelabra of yellow flowers surges upwards to create an unmissable display.

can enjoy their rosettes in the garden from late autumn into spring and, when they flower, they open a little earlier and bloom far more prolifically.

The challenge, of course, is choosing neighbors that complement the rosettes at flowering time. Better split the task: settling on dwarf bulbs as spring companions and early summer-flowering perennials for later is a wise option.

## Spring shoots/summer flowers

Foliage and flowers are the familiar features for which we select perennials, but another significant attraction, restricted to a time of year when its color is especially valuable, is their emerging spring shoots. Red, smoky purple, electric green, sheathed in rusty scales—the list is long.

Sometimes a whole genus complies, but often it is important to select a particular species or cultivar that exhibits this feature. The new spring foliage of almost every columbine is fresh and attractive, while with peonies some are far more vivid than others, so a careful choice must be made. With pokeweeds, the emerging shoots of the variegated *Phytolacca americana* 'Melody' and 'Silberstein' are more interestingly colored than those of the wild form.

▼ The fresh spring foliage of columbines looks well with the slender leaves and bright flowers of daffodils and will spread to hide the daffodil foliage as it fades.

Introduction

Later, as the columbines and peonies come into flower, a quite different set of choices must be made, for now the plants that began the season as a cluster of crimson shoots or a dome of fresh foliage around which smaller plants could be grouped bloom boldly, and the color and style of these flowers must connect with the plants around them.

Planting must be dense to capitalize on these features, and we must encourage thriving, dense growth by tending the soil and the plants thoughtfully. Both irrigation, when necessary, and planting in good soil help grow more plants in one area than you might normally attempt.

## Winter bark/fall foliage color

If invaluable fall foliage color can be shown off by trees that also feature signature winter bark, then we have a coupling to dominate when spring and summer's excesses are passed and faded. Trees with bark that is colorful, or even strikingly patterned, shine in the winter garden, just when we need them most. Spring and summer's color distracts and dominates, then as the fall foliage blows away, their bark's light and color again emerges. Some gardeners even go out with a bucket and brush and scrub the bark clean as winter approaches.

Many trees feature bark which

▼ ▽ The pink early growth of *Phytolacca americana* 'Silberstein' is followed by variegated foliage, white flowers, and then strings of berries like blackcurrants.

▽ ▼ The combination of beautifully patterned bark, especially appreciated in winter, and multicolored fall foliage is a feature of many fine trees, including this *Stewartia pseudocamellia*.

reveals fascinating patterns or a delicate coloring when inspected closely. But, in some climates, we admire the winter effect of these trees more from the window than the path, so bold coloring and the right background is important.

Birches, cherries, and maples are the leaders in supplying what we need, but choosing precisely the correct form is crucial. In all these groups, a hurried choice may leave you with a tree whose bark is undistinguished or whose fall color is feeble and fleeting.

## Changing foliage

Even if a plant never flowers, never contributing anything to the garden except its leaves, it can still be valuable. For the leaves of some plants, both evergreen and deciduous, change as the year rolls round. Heucheras, heucherellas, and tiarellas are especially valuable in this respect, with an unexpected range of changing tones, but think also of other perennials, and shrubs and trees. Japanese maples (*Acer palmatum*) often feature prettily divided or dissected foliage from spring into fall; many are worth growing for that feature alone, then in fall take on fiery color. Many conifers develop rustier or orange coloring in winter.

Some lady ferns (*Athyrium*) and others change color as the season progresses. Especially appealing are the hybrids whose coloring intensifies through the season, while other ferns develop bright fall color. Some hostas—whatever their summer color—develop autumnal biscuit brown and bright yellow tones; some mukdenias are reddish bronze as they emerge, then turn green, then develop crimson coloring, especially at the tips.

## Evergreens with extras

Conifers, variegated hollies, ceanothus, and Mediterranean spurges are a valuable and appealing presence in the garden simply through the coloring and shape of their attractive—and ever-present—leaves. But at specific seasons they add to their beauty an extra feature. Conifers obviously bring cones and, while many are undistinguished, some are spectacular.

▶ ▷ *Mukdenia rossii*, a saxifrage relative whose foliage moves through a succession of colors, also features spikes of white spring flowers.

▷ ▶ Fall color from four plants (with highlights of other seasons noted): *Acer palmatum* (prettily divided summer foliage), *A. griseum* (winter bark), *Syringa meyeri* 'Palibin' (spring flowers), and *Physocarpus opulifolius* 'Coppertina' ('Mindia') (coppery spring foliage).

The small white flowers of hollies line their branches in spring but, more importantly, these are followed by red, orange, or yellow berries, which ripen in fall, not only creating an impressive color combination with the variegated foliage but also attracting feeding birds. Variegated ceanothus, on the other hand, boast powdery heads of blue flowers in spring or summer, and the combination of the yellow-edged deep green foliage and the blue flowers always attracts comment.

The variegated forms of Mediterranean spurges, with their blue-gray or green leaves edged in white or cream, make an impact all year round, often on imposing plants. Then in spring, these evergreen euphorbias are topped with fat heads of small greenish yellow, white, or even variegated flowers, which harmonize well with the leaves, but in a different style.

## Choose carefully

One of the surprising conclusions coming from thinking about multi-season plants is the realization of how many there are, and with what combinations of features:

- Winter bark/spring flowers/fall foliage color
- Winter stems/spring flowers/fall fruits
- Spring shoots/summer foliage/fall flowers
- Summer flowers/fall foliage color
- Summer foliage/fall foliage color

But simply noting that I have *Euphorbia* or *Viburnum*, for example, amongst my choices in the A-to-Z entries is not an assertion that all their forms are blessed with the features valued in this book.

For even as we all become more thoughtful and sophisticated in the way we think about our gardens and more demanding in what, precisely, we expect from our plants, so also must we choose our plants more carefully, and with more precision. Just any old hosta, rose, dahlia, or witch hazel won't do—as a preliminary dip into each genus, by way of example, demonstrates.

*Hosta* 'Great Expectations' has far more appeal than simply the bold and impressive foliage of so many other varieties; by early summer it

▶ When mature, Britain's favorite Christmas tree, Norway spruce (*Picea abies*), produces the longest and most impressive cones of any spruce.

has already gone through two transformations. The emerging shoots, hazed in purple, yellow, and cream at first, catch the eye when just a few inches tall. Then, with the first hints of the slug-resistant, seersuckered leaves peeping out and unfurling, their coloring begins to reveal itself. A month later, in its glory, a brilliant yellow splash shines out from each

◀ *Hosta* 'Great Expectations' develops a succession of appealing features which reinforce the idea that, chosen well, hostas can provide far more than simply bold foliage.

The grayish foliage of *Rosa glauca*, with its intriguing red tints, is the perfect background for the white-eyed pink flowers. In autumn, when the flowers and foliage have passed, the tangle of stems carries bright orange-red hips.

blue-green leaf. That's not all: a little more than two months after emerging—there are the flowers, almost white, though sadly unscented, and held on white stems. The color combination is not ideal, but you can always cut them for the house.

Although 'Great Expectations' can make a dramatic specimen, it is not quick growing so is ideal in a small garden, where it is more likely to be subject to special attention in the form of watering and feeding—and appreciation.

Roses are a more obvious example of the need to choose exactly the right varieties to ensure at least a two-for-one contribution to the garden. Most roses do one thing and do it supremely well: they bloom, either in an exuberant burst in early summer, or in a long and continuous flow of flower into the autumn. In many their fragrance is an added appeal. But there are a few which feature both colorful flowers in summer and red hips in the fall; some also bring us colorful fall foliage. But only a handful

provide attractive foliage all summer *and* flowers *and* fruits. *Rosa glauca* is the prime example.

Its winter shoots are reddish brown, with only a very few thorns, then in spring the foliage opens and its coloring is unique: grayish green, with a hint of purple in shady situations and the addition of coppery tones in sun. The new stems are also purplish, and coppery purple buds open to single pink flowers with the central boss of yellow anthers backed by a white disk. Later, in fall, the foliage often turns plum-colored, and there are rounded red hips that last for many weeks. So instead of the one colorful feature of most roses, *Rosa glauca* offers a succession of features at different times of the year: winter stems, spring and summer foliage and stems, early summer flowers, fall foliage color, and autumn and winter fruits.

For two or three months of summer color that hits you between the eyes, look no further than dahlias. With dramatically double flowers up to 12in/30cm across in almost every color you can think off except true blue, dahlias are unbeatable. But the savvy gardener has other ideas: do they do anything else? And the answer is that most do nothing else at all—but oh, the dark-leaved forms. The Happy Single series of dahlias from Holland offers elegant single flowers in almost a dozen different colors, including some intriguing bicolors, held on relatively short and manageable plants—ideal in large containers and good towards the front of sunny borders. What makes them desirable multi-season plants is that from the moment the new foliage opens, the leaves are rich reddish bronze in color. They mature bronze with greenish tints but, essentially, they impress both as foliage plants and flowering plants. All have names associated with being happy and unattached.

Finally, the Asian witch hazels, *Hamamelis mollis* and its hybrid *H. ×intermedia*, are essential winter and early spring flowering shrubs that combine a number of valuable features—but in varying combinations. Many have an elegant habit of growth, some spreading and some more upright, but almost always attractive; most flower well; some are scented; some feature yellow and/or orange and/or red fall foliage color. The trick is to choose varieties that combine as many of these features as possible—and preferably all of them.

But consider: 'Aphrodite', 'Diana', 'Glowing Embers', 'Jelena', 'Rubin', and 'Sunburst' have no scent or hardly any scent. 'Aphrodite', 'Glowing Embers', and 'Sunburst' have no fall leaf color, or hardly any. 'Jelena' has great flower color and superb fall foliage color so is worth growing just for that combination. But why grow 'Aphrodite', 'Glowing Embers', or 'Sunburst' unless you have enough space to grow every hamamelis there is and want to complete your collection?

The five powerhouse stars are 'Arnold Promise', 'Aurora', 'Pallida', 'Vesna', and 'Wisley Supreme', all of which combine generous flowering, strong fragrance, and fine fall color.

In short, it pays to hunt for the best varieties. So take a look at my choices of excellent plants in the pages that follow. And again, remember my mantra whenever you are deciding on a new plant for your garden: "What else does it do?"

▶ ▷ The Happy Single series of dahlias features attractive bronze foliage and a wide range of flower colors including (clockwise from top left) 'Flame' ('HS Flame'), 'First Love' ('HS First Love'), 'Date' ('HS Date'), and 'Single Party' ('HS Party').

▷ ▶ Despite its weak fragrance, *Hamamelis* ×*intermedia* 'Jelena' is worth growing for its marmalade-colored flowers and its fiery autumn color.

# A TO Z OF
# POWERHOUSE
# PLANTS

# abelia

**evergreen shrub**

- *evergreen foliage*
- *spring shoots*
- *summer and fall flowers*

*Unbeatable combination of glossy leaves and colorful late-season flowers*

All abelias are valuable, especially in smaller gardens, but the variegated forms are especially rewarding. In spring, the new shoots open with strong pink coloring, which may rival the flowers for brightness. Then, until winter, there is glossy foliage, rich green and colorfully variegated, and in mid or late summer and into the autumn the flowers arrive—and the whole flower cluster is colorful. The buds are usually dark pink pearls, even before the blooms open. Then the trumpet-shaped flowers come in white, or shades of pink and lilac, and amongst them the bracts (miniature leaves) are slightly bronzed or reddish like the buds. An impressive catalog of features. And their attractive, often arching, rather twiggy growth is easily manageable.

*Abelia ×grandiflora* 'Hopleys' is my pick. Its foliage is outstandingly well colored, opening with vivid yellow margins to the dark green leaves, contrasting brightly with the red stems, and fading to an appropriately harmonious creamy white by flowering time. The prolific lavender pink flowers open in succession for many weeks. 'Hopleys' scores over other variegated forms for a number of reasons: the harmonious coloring of pale flowers and creamy leaf edges is outstanding; it never throws plain green shoots, which would soon take over the plant; and its growth is conveniently neater than many, with an engagingly spreading habit.

But there are others, and these too are good. 'Golden Anniversary' ('Minipan') has yellow-edged leaves and red stems; 'Silver Anniversary' ('Panache') has silver- or cream-edged foliage. Both are more compact than 'Hopleys'. 'Kaleidoscope' stands out for its coppery fresh shoots, long flowering season, and outstanding reddish fall leaves, which, for the rest of the year, are dark green edged with yellow.

▶ Early in the season the new yellow-edged foliage of 'Hopleys' is dominant; later, the lavender pink flowers from darker buds and pale creamy variegation make a winning summer combination.

## ESSENTIALS

• Mature abelias make good hosts for less vigorous clematis. Many also make superb long-term container specimens.

• Happy in any reasonably fertile soil, in full sun or partial shade. In areas where abelias are marginally hardy, grow them on walls for extra protection or move their containers to a protected place in winter.

• Prune in spring for the most prolific display, but abelias flower well without pruning. If they grow too tall, they respond well even to unskilled pruning. If cut back by winter cold, cut away any dead growth in spring; they usually spring up again as temperatures rise. Rarely troubled by pests or diseases.

*Abelia ×grandiflora* **'Golden Anniversary' ('Minipan')**
Z6–9
24–28 × 24–28in
60–70 × 60–70cm

*Abelia ×grandiflora* **'Hopleys'**
Z7–9
4–6 × 6–8ft
1.2–1.8 × 1.8–2.4m

*Abelia ×grandiflora* **'Kaleidoscope'**
Z6–9
2–3 × 3–4ft
0.6–0.9 × 0.9–1.2m

*Abelia ×grandiflora* **'Silver Anniversary' ('Panache')**
Z6–9
24–28 × 24–28in
60–70 × 60–70cm

▲ The coppery young foliage of 'Kaleidoscope' gives way to green-centered yellow leaves and pink buds, which open to almost white. Reddish coloring returns in fall.

# maple

**deciduous tree**

Most maples color brightly in the fall. The North American forests are ablaze with them, and in gardens across the temperate world they are required planting for their fiery fall tones. But some have an invaluable second feature: beautiful winter bark, in a variety of colors and patterns. And all these are, very conveniently, rather modest in size so cannot be excluded from most gardens on the grounds that they will overdominate. All have common names that neatly describe their main bark feature.

*Acer griseum* (paperbark maple), a Chinese species, has cinnamon-colored bark which peels and rolls back to reveal brighter coloring underneath. The newly uncovered bark is more red or more orange in tone, weathering to cinnamon

- *winter bark*
- *spring flowers*
- *summer foliage and fruits*
- *fall foliage color*

*Choose wisely for a choice pairing of good fall color and beautiful winter bark*

◀ The paperbark maple, *A. griseum,* features attractive peeling bark, even on young specimens, and softly fiery fall color.

shades, so that a delicate range of colors is shown off. Specimens of paperbark maples that branch relatively low down offer the most impressive sight, as the multiple limbs provide varying examples of the peeling bark. Branched trunks offer a more direct appeal and, while without the impact of more mature specimens, even the bark of relatively young trees will be noticed once the leaves have fallen. In fall, those leaves turn shades of red and orange and yellow, almost as if the whole tree had been lit with a match.

The snakebark maples, natives of China and North America, have a very different winter look. Dark green bark is striped along its length in pale green and white or even pink; in a few cases, the background green coloring is almost completely covered in pale streaks.

The striped maple, *A. pensylvanicum*, is widespread all over eastern North America. It is one of the first trees to spring up in cleared forest—if the deer are fenced out—and some foresters regard it as a weed, as it can dominate the understory. The current season's twigs are yellowish green but turn green in their first winter. After a few years they become irregularly striped in white. The fall color is lovely, uniform clear gold, and there is also a third feature: the 4–6in/10–15cm strings of bright yellow late spring flowers. 'Erythrocladum', with very bright, reddish pink white-striped shoots and bark, is a variety that divides opinion sharply: some see the intense coloring as overkill, others as captivating.

From Asia come two species similar to *A. pensylvanicum*: *A. capillipes* and *A. grosseri*. *Acer capillipes* has the same green and white striped bark as well as coral-colored new shoots, red leaf stalks, and red and orange fall color. *Acer grosseri* var. *hersii* is probably the pick, with bark more marbled than striped and bright scarlet fall foliage.

The coral bark maple, *A. palmatum* 'Sango-kaku' ('Senkaki'), is slightly different, one of the very best trees for small spaces and ideal as the only tree in a very small garden. Although the color of the oldest branches is unremarkable, twigs and maturing branches are a vivid coral pink-red, a shade especially appealing in winter when seen against snow or a blue sky. The neat, five-lobed leaves are a lovely fresh green and in fall turn soft yellow, making an unmistakable pairing with the bark—even after frost has dropped them

## ESSENTIALS

- Site paperbark and snakebark maples where their patterning can be admired: near paths, near windows where they can be seen from inside in winter, and against simple backgrounds. Shelter from wind and early frost will help prolong fall color.

- All are happy in any reasonable soil (although neither shallow, chalky soils nor dry conditions are suitable), and in full sun to partial shade. The coral bark maple prefers a neutral to a slightly acid soil and a site shaded from midday sun to prevent leaf scorch.

- No pruning except to remove dead or damaged branches. Preventing children from tearing the bark from *A. griseum* is prudent, and a gentle washdown and light scrub on a mild, late fall day will bring out its color beautifully.

◀ Changing seasons in the red spectrum, 'Red Dragon' is at its deepest color in summer and is electric bright in spring and fall.

to the ground around the tree in a sunny carpet.

There are many other Japanese maples (*A. palmatum*) with attractively green or purple leaves, some lacily divided, as well as purplish spring flowers and red-winged summer fruits, and they too boast fall foliage in fiery tones. 'Bloodgood' makes a small tree with dark purple leaves turning red in the fall. 'Inaba-shidare' has very finely cut purplish leaves on red stalks, turning crimson and coral red in fall, and is especially good in hot climates. The foliage of 'Red Dragon' is bold but changes in a more subtle way, from bright scarlet in spring to deep burgundy to flaming red in fall.

Finally two forms of *A. negundo*, the box elder or ash-leaved maple, are grown for their young shoots and cut down hard in spring, in the same way as some dogwoods, to promote strong, well-colored winter stems. 'Winter Lightning' is bright green, var. *violaceum* is purple, and both feature large, bold, ash-like foliage in summer.

▲ The American native *A. pensylvanicum* has attractively striped bark, colorful new twigs, and soft gold fall color.

▶ 'Winter Lightning' will make a tall tree if left unpruned; cut it back hard every spring to promote this surge of stiff twiggy growth. Bold foliage follows.

*Acer capillipes*
Z5–8
30 × 30ft
9 × 9m

*Acer griseum*
Z4–8
30 × 30ft
9 × 9m

*Acer grosseri* var. *hersii*
Z5–8
50 × 50ft
15 × 15m

*Acer negundo* var. *violaceum*
Z5–8
6–8 × 6–8ft
1.8–2.4 × 1.8–2.4m when
pruned annually

*Acer negundo* 'Winter
Lightning'
Z5–8
6–8 × 6–8ft
1.8–2.4 × 1.8–2.4m when
pruned annually

*Acer palmatum* 'Bloodgood'
Z6–8
15 × 15ft
4.5 × 4.5m

*Acer palmatum* 'Inaba-shidare'
Z4–8
5 × 8ft
1.5 × 2.4m

*Acer palmatum* 'Red Dragon'
Z6–8
5.5–8 × 8–10ft
1.7–2.4 × 2.4–3m

*Acer palmatum* 'Sango-kaku'
('Senkaki')
Z6–8
20 × 15ft
6 × 4.5m

*Acer pensylvanicum*
Z3–7
40 × 30ft
12 × 9m

*Acer pensylvanicum* 'Erythrocladum'
Z3–7
40 × 30ft
12 × 9m

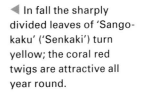

◀ In fall the sharply
divided leaves of 'Sango-
kaku' ('Senkaki') turn
yellow; the coral red
twigs are attractive all
year round.

## *Actaea*

# bugbane, baneberry

**perennial**

- *spring shoots*
- *spring or summer flowers*
- *summer foliage and fruits*

*Powerhouse plants with a quartet of assets for borders and shade gardens*

The botanists have been busy with these plants recently, and what we used to know as *Cimicifuga* (bugbane, cohosh) has now been united with *Actaea* (baneberry). Some nurseries still use *Cimicifuga* but, increasingly, all are to be found under *Actaea*.

The baneberries are valuable American native shade lovers with distinct contributions in early spring, late spring, and summer. In *A. rubra*, for example, the first sign of their presence is the spring surge of pale bronze, fleshy new shoots, with leaves rolled over tightly at the tip. In a few days, as the stems stretch, the clustered buds become visible, still in bronzed tones with hints of

▶ ▷ With its fluffy heads of white flowers followed by gleaming red berries, *A. rubra* is a surprising plant for shade, intriguing in even its early stages.

▷ ▶ 'Black Negligee' has especially dark foliage and carries long flower spikes.

## ESSENTIALS

- Site the berrying types where their new shoots can be appreciated and where neighbors will expand to fill their space in late summer and fall. Site tall foliage types towards the back of the border, but ensure their early foliage is not hidden.

- Both types appreciate at least some shade and a rich, fertile soil that does not dry out; both generally dislike lime.

- Cut berrying types back in late summer when the foliage and berries are past their best; leave foliage types till after flowering later in fall.

green, then growth extends and expands rapidly. Soon the fresh green, sharply toothed foliage is unfurling—an ideal background for the more or less rounded heads of fluffy white flowers.

There follows a phase when the elegant, repeatedly divided fresh green foliage is the main feature. Then the fruits start to color, and in *A. rubra* these are bright and shining glossy scarlet. The fruiting heads can be so heavy as to weigh the stems down to the horizontal, which, frankly, is unfortunate; but discreet support of the lower part of the stems with slender canes will solve the problem. There is also a form with white berries known correctly as *A. rubra* f. *neglecta* but also listed as f. *leucocarpa*, var. *alba*, and even *A. alba*.

*Actaea pachypoda*, often known by the common name of doll's eyes, is broadly similar but features bright white berries with purple tips held on red stalks. Just to confuse the issue, not only are there the aforementioned white-berried forms of *A. rubra*, but there are red-berried forms of *A. pachypoda*!

Plants formerly gathered in *Cimicifuga* are much more substantial and, although without the benefit of colorful fruits, they benefit from purple

or bronze foliage. All are forms of *A. simplex*, an Asian woodlander that can reach astonishing heights in flower when grown in rich, moist soil. As the leaves of these dark forms emerge they may be deep purple or bronze, or softened attractively with green tints; the foliage then expands into a bold mass of leaves, each leaf repeatedly divided and, at its best, richly colored but often greening later. (I should point out that nurseries use words like "bronze," "purple," and "mahogany" with an unhelpful lack of precision, and that the amount of sun and moisture influences foliage color.) The dark flower stems strike up through the foliage, and in late summer and autumn the dark purplish buds open to densely packed spikes of fluffy pink or white flowers. They are usually, sometimes strongly, fragrant.

Atropurpurea Group is the name used to cover dark-leaved selections of *A. simplex* raised from seed. Although these all feature dark leaves and fragrant white flowers, plants can vary significantly in the coloring of their stems, foliage, and flower buds, so it pays to choose plants under this name in the nursery and not trust to mail order.

'Black Negligee' is more vigorous than most and features

dark stems carrying very dark foliage setting off the unusually long flower spikes.

'Brunette' has stems and foliage stained purplish red. The flower spikes bend over strongly at the tips, and each purplish pink flower bud opens to strongly scented, pink-tinted white flowers.

'Hillside Black Beauty' has purplish red stems and leaves and erect flower stems, on which purple buds open to white, heavily scented flowers.

'James Compton' has tall purple stems with a slightly bluish tint and purplish red foliage that is a little paler than that of other varieties. The erect spikes carry purplish buds, which open to strongly fragrant white flowers.

'Pink Spike' is the best form for pink flowers, which open white from purplish buds. The purple-tinted green young shoots retain that blend as they mature; the branched stems carry slightly arched flower spikes thick with bloom.

▲ The purplish buds of 'Pink Spike' open to white flowers, which soon blush pink. The purple-tinted green leaves retain their color from spring into autumn.

*Actaea pachypoda*
   Z4–9
   24–36 × 18–24in
   60–90 × 45–60cm

*Actaea rubra*
   Z4–8
   18–24 × 12–18in
   45–60 × 30–45cm

*Actaea rubra* f. *neglecta*
   Z4–8
   18–24 × 12–18in
   45–60 × 30–45cm

*Actaea simplex* Atropurpurea
   Group
   Z4–8
   4–7 × 2–4ft
   1.2–2.1 × 0.6–1.2m

*Actaea simplex* 'Black Negligee'
   Z4–8
   4–5 × 2–3ft
   1.2–1.5 × 0.6–0.9m

*Actaea simplex* 'Brunette'
   Z4–8
   4–7 × 2–4ft
   1.2–2.1 × 0.6–1.2m

*Actaea simplex* 'Hillside Black
   Beauty'
   Z4–8
   4–7 × 2–4ft
   1.2–2.1 × 0.6–1.2m

*Actaea simplex* 'James
   Compton'
   Z4–8
   5–7 × 2–4ft
   1.5–2.1 × 0.6–1.2m

*Actaea simplex* 'Pink Spike'
   Z4–8
   4–5 × 2–3ft
   1.2–1.5 × 0.6–0.9m

▲ The white-fruited form
of *A. rubra*, f. *neglecta*,
looks well against the rich
green foliage.

# narrow leaf blue star   *Amsonia*

**perennial**

Discovered in 1942 by mala-cologist Leslie Hubricht, on a snail-hunting expedition to Arkansas, *A. hubrichtii* is the only species in this genus of sixteen drought-tolerant southern U.S. natives to qualify as a powerhouse plant. Even before it flowers, it makes an attractive mound of very narrow, almost thread-like, deep green leaves. Then, at the tip of each shoot, clusters of blue buds (darker blue at

- *summer flowers*
- *fall foliage color*

*One award-winning species stands out in this drought-tolerant genus*

◀ The five-pointed blue stars of *A. hubrichtii* top every shoot and become paler as temperatures rise.

## ESSENTIALS

- Pair with a bronze-leaved weigela or physocarpus; these or similar pairings work in summer, with the amsonia's blue-tinted flowers and rich green foliage, and in fall, as the amsonia turns on the sunshine.

- Best in full sun, in any reasonable soil; it will grow in partial shade but may not color up so well in fall. It seems to me when the plant is raised from seed, as it usually is, both the flower color and the fall foliage transition varies slightly from plant to plant. Drought tolerant when established and unexpectedly hardy, considering this species grows naturally in Arkansas and Oklahoma: it will take −20F/−29C.

- Cut back down to the ground in late fall, once the color is gone, or in early spring.

◀ The vivid, bright yellow fall color of *A. hubrichtii* is outstanding amongst all hardy perennials, and its slender foliage gives it a delicate, airy look.

the base) appear and open to starry pale blue flowers. As temperatures rise, the flowers turn paler, becoming almost white in some climates. The flowers develop into long, slim pods filled with seeds shaped like tiny nails.

Through the summer the almost effervescent mound of slender green foliage is, well, if not a feature then certainly attractive. But in fall everything changes, and the whole plant is transformed as the foliage turns from green, to green with golden tints, to bright buttercup yellow, to coppery gold. This is the sort of stunning color that sends

you into a ditch as you drive round the corner: it grabs your attention and won't let go. Please, gardeners, do not plant it at the roadside. If you do, someone will surely crash into your fence.

The flowers of some other species may be more colorful, but the fall color is less reliable and much less intense; in *A. ciliata*, with even narrower foliage, the fall color is excellent but flowering is disappointing, and it can be difficult to find in nurseries. Narrow leaf blue star, named Perennial Plant of the Year in 2011, really is the star amongst blue stars.

*Amsonia ciliata*
Z6–10
2–3 × 2–3ft
0.6–0.9 × 0.6–0.9m

*Amsonia hubrichtii*
Z6–8
3 × 4ft
0.9 × 1.2m

## *Antirrhinum*

# snapdragon

**annual**

- *spring to fall foliage*
- *summer flowers*

*Traditional garden favorite, now with even more arresting foliage*

Snapdragons are flowers that everyone seems to enjoy, in ways as various as pinching the sides of the flowers to make their "mouths" open to gathering them in cottage-style arrangements for the house. But when not in bloom, plants were unremarkable—until varieties with colored or variegated foliage came along in the 1800s.

The first such antique was 'Black Prince', which although never widely grown has stayed in catalogs all these years. Its foliage is deep purple bronze, a sultry coloring that is rare amongst annuals, from the emergence of the new seedlings to the opening of the deep crimson flowers. Then, as the buds form, a green haze begins to infiltrate, but those blood red flowers open and a harmonious pairing of colors is created. In a similar vein is 'Night and Day': same deep and dark foliage, but the flowers are scarlet crimson with a white tube—a startling combination.

Both 'Black Prince' and 'Night and Day' are tall enough to cut for the house. 'Bronze Dragon' is more for containers or edging; deep purple, not bronze, the foliage is topped by short spikes of pale, almost white, flowers with dark pink lips, making a very pretty combination. All are raised from seed and provide an attractive summer display, even in Alaska, while in almost frost-free areas they may survive the winter for another season of color.

Two recently introduced varieties, not raised from seed, offer brightly variegated foliage. Pink-flowered 'Eternal' and 'Snapdaddy Yellow' look more imposing than earlier, weaker variegated types and branch well from the base. Their slightly grayish green foliage is edged in creamy white, making a soft harmonious combination, beautiful even without flowers.

▶ 'Bronze Dragon', one of several dark-leaved snapdragons, looks good for many weeks before the flowers open.

## ESSENTIALS

- Plant with low, bushy annuals such as lobelias and begonias. 'Black Prince' looks stunning with the limey yellow leaves of *Helichrysum petiolare* 'Limelight'. Variegated sorts are good with *Ipomoea* 'Blackie' and other dark-leaved sweet potatoes.

- Best in sunshine and in fertile but well-drained soil.

- Deadhead as the flowers fade. Taller types may need support. Technically perennials, but when grown as annuals for summer display, it pays to start afresh each year. Rarely seen in nurseries, unfortunately; most are raised from seed.

▶ The white-edged, grayish foliage of 'Eternal' makes a colorful clump before the pink snapdragons open.

*Antirrhinum* 'Black Prince'
  Z8–9
  18 × 12in
  45 × 30cm

*Antirrhinum* 'Bronze Dragon'
  Z8–9
  10–12 × 6–9in
  25–30 × 15–23cm

*Antirrhinum* 'Eternal'
  Z8–9
  18 × 12in
  45 × 30cm

*Antirrhinum* 'Night and Day'
  Z8–9
  18 × 12in
  45 × 30cm

*Antirrhinum* 'Snapdaddy Yellow'
  Z8–9
  18 × 12in
  45 × 30cm

# columbine

## *Aquilegia*

**perennial**

The emerging foliage of columbines, especially after rain, is one of the delights of the spring garden. Every columbine I have ever seen has had that special early appeal: the new foliage is soft and fresh, the water droplets hang around the edge. Some columbines, including the red columbine (*A. canadensis*), reveal a rich red haze as the leaves open, which then fades away. But even in plain green, they appeal.

Later, one of two things happens. In most columbines the foliage expands into an elegant green mound. In a few, more colorful foliage develops—yellow, gold, or with golden or cream variegations—and as the foliage expands and

- *spring and summer foliage*
- *spring and summer flowers*

*Delightful new spring foliage followed by a rainbow of colorful flowers*

◀ In many columbines, the new spring growth is both prettily divided and delightfully colored—raindrops are a frequent bonus.

## ESSENTIALS

- Those with pretty new foliage are best towards the front of the border, with daffodils, whose dying leaves the expanding foliage will hide. Double-flowered and mottled forms also need a frontal position. Those with yellow or gold foliage can be farther back in the border, as their impact is less subtle. They too make good neighbors for early bulbs.

- Happy in most reasonably fertile soils in full sun or a little shade. In containers, keep moist and feed regularly.

- Columbines often thrive for only two or three years. Pinching out flower stems in their first year will help give them a longer life and ensure foliage looks its best. Watch for leaf miner (nip off the affected leaves) and caterpillars (pick them off or squash them).

◀ The richly mottled foliage of 'Woodside Gold' looks good in the border or in a container.

develops, the coloring becomes more striking. Then, in spring and early summer, the flowers appear—single or in a range of compelling double forms, in almost every color and color combination. Some are fragrant; many have impressive impact.

Vervaeneana Group is the general name that covers all forms of or hybrids involving *A. vulgaris* with yellow and green mottled foliage—whatever the flower color. 'Burnished Rose' has rich golden foliage and pinkish red, granny's bonnet flowers; the leaves of 'Roman Bronze' emerge yellow, darkening to bronzy orange and then, when the fragrant, violet-blue flowers open, turn almost green; 'Mellow

*Aquilegia canadensis*
Z3–8
18–36 × 12–15in
45–90 × 30–38cm

*Aquilegia* 'Roman Bronze'
Z3–8
24–36 × 15–18in
60–90 × 38–45cm

*Aquilegia vulgaris* 'Burnished Rose'
Z3–8
24–36 × 15–18in
60–90 × 38–45cm

*Aquilegia vulgaris* 'Mellow Yellow'
Z3–8
24–36 × 15–18in
60–90 × 38–45cm

Yellow' has soft yellow foliage and white flowers; 'Woodside Gold' has mottled foliage and blue or violet flowers, 'Woodside Mixed' has mottled foliage and flowers in white and in red, pink, and blue shades, 'Woodside White' has mottled foliage and white or pale blue flowers.

Most columbines are grown in borders, but those with gold or mottled foliage also make fine container plants. These varieties tend to develop into substantial plants in their first year and bloom in the second. Grow them from spring-sown seed yourself and they rarely flower until their second year, but in that first year they make invaluable foliage plants.

*Aquilegia vulgaris* Vervaeneana Group
Z3–8
24–36 × 15–18in
60–90 × 38–45cm

*Aquilegia vulgaris* 'Woodside Gold'
Z3–8
24–36 × 15–18in
60–90 × 38–45cm

*Aquilegia vulgaris* 'Woodside Mixed'
Z3–8
24–36 × 15–18in
60–90 × 38–45cm

*Aquilegia vulgaris* 'Woodside White'
Z3–8
24–36 × 15–18in
60–90 × 38–45cm

## *Bergenia*

# elephant's ear

**perennial**

- *winter foliage*
- *spring flowers*
- *summer foliage*

*Bold winter foliage gives way to attractive weed-smothering summer leaves*

Bergenias would be worth growing for their winter and summer foliage even if they never flowered in between. The broad, rounded, leathery, often slightly pleated, evergreen foliage of most bergenias rises almost directly from the roots and standing up almost vertically can look like a flotilla of sailboats drifting across the border. As winter approaches and conditions cool, the best develop bronzed, purplish, crimson or even bright red tones, which are invaluable through the winter. In snowy areas, the richly colored foliage may be the first to be revealed by the retreating snow.

In spring, the slightly succulent flower stalks emerge between the leaves and carry flowers in white, magenta, or a wide variety of vivid and delicate pink shades. In the best, the flowers are carried just above the leaves; in the worst, the leaves hide them. When the flowers fade, brilliantly glossy new foliage emerges, gleaming in the summer sun and developing into a very effective ground cover. The trick is to choose the forms that combine the best winter foliage with the best spring flowers and the best summer foliage to give us a three-season, weed-smothering perennial.

'Bressingham Ruby' has deep ruby wine foliage in winter, reddish pink flowers in spring, and rich green summer foliage with red tints. It is also compact and its growth is not too dense, so early dwarf bulbs can emerge between the leaves. 'Cabernet' is popular in the States and has purplish red winter foliage, vivid pink spring flowers on red stems, and bright green summer leaves. 'Eric Smith' is always impressive in winter, but the color seems to vary from almost scarlet to wine red. The flowers are vivid pink, and the summer foliage deep green. The old-timer 'Pugsley's Pink' has enormous branched flowerheads, wine-tinted green winter foliage, and green summer leaves.

▶ The overwintered foliage of 'Bressingham Ruby' is a colorful mixture of green, red, and purple tones.

nurseries and garden centers— but this is a splendid plant. The bark is bright white, the growth rather upright, and the fall color is warm gold. Lovely. If you prefer more exceptional forms, hunt down 'Grayswood Ghost' (the brightest brilliant white bark), 'Jermyns' (bright white bark, unusually long catkins), or 'Silver Shadow' (very bright white bark). Two others to look out for are *B. albosinensis* var. *septentrionalis* (grayish pink bark) and *B. ermanii* (creamy pink bark).

There are also impressive forms from North America and Europe. Two North American native species stand out. *Betula nigra*, especially its form 'Heritage', features

## ESSENTIALS

• Birches cast only light shade, so encourage a wide range of shade plants to grow below. Many never reach their stated maximum height. Try to plant them against an evergreen background, so their color is shown off well.

• Happy in full sun, or a little shade; some birches appreciate moisture, some like it drier, so check individual species.

• Stake well when planting; do not attempt to "improve" their shape by pruning; scrub the bark with soapy water after leaf fall.

◀ ◁ The bright white bark of *B. utilis* var. *jacquemontii* stands out well against a background of rhododendrons.

◁ ◀ The bark of *B. albosinensis* var. *septentrionalis* is its highlight, but there are also spring catkins and yellow fall color.

shaggy bark in pink and orange tones, while the bark of *B. alleghaniensis* is a more honey or golden brown shade; it features yellow spring catkins and spectacular fall color. From Europe comes *B. pendula*; its cut-leaved form 'Laciniata' features an elegant weeping habit, white bark, and yellow fall color. 'Youngii' is more narrowly weeping and suited to even smaller spaces than most birches.

While Asian birches are popular on both sides of the Atlantic, American species are often passed over in Europe and European species ignored in North America. It should not be so.

*Betula albosinensis* var. *septentrionalis*
Z5–8
80 × 30ft
25 × 9m

*Betula alleghaniensis*
Z4–8
80 × 30ft
25 × 9m

*Betula ermanii*
Z5–8
70 × 40ft
21 × 12m

*Betula nigra*
Z4–9
60 × 40ft
18 × 12m

*Betula nigra* 'Heritage'
Z4–9
60 × 40ft
18 × 12m

*Betula pendula*
Z2–8
80 × 30ft
25 × 9m

*Betula pendula* 'Laciniata'
Z2–8
30 × 10ft
9 × 3m

*Betula pendula* 'Youngii'
Z2–8
25 × 10ft
8 × 3m

*Betula utilis* var. *jacquemontii*
Z5–8
60 × 30ft
18 × 9m

*Betula utilis* var. *jacquemontii* 'Grayswood Ghost'
Z5–8
60 × 30ft
18 × 9m

*Betula utilis* var. *jacquemontii* 'Jermyns'
Z5–8
60 × 30ft
18 × 9m

*Betula utilis* var. *jacquemontii* 'Silver Shadow'
Z5–8
60 × 30ft
18 × 9m

# false forget-me-not     *Brunnera*

**perennial**

The unimproved *B. macrophylla* is an extremely useful species for difficult situations but is largely unblessed by features that would suggest it as a powerhouse plant. True, the leaves are broad and bold, similar to those of a hosta, but rough, and with a scattering of a few silvery spots; blue or white flowers, like tiny forget-me-nots, are produced in spring. So this is an effective, largely utilitarian plant, making efficient weed-smothering ground cover in many situations, including dry and poor soil. However, there are many forms whose foliage is attractively marked, and so the best brunneras fit into the valuable class of plants with attractive foliage from spring to fall, with an additional flurry of flowers. In each variety that follows, the cloud of dainty bright blue flowers comes in spring.

These chosen varieties are especially effective as container plants. Start with three small plants in a 12 or 15in/30 or 38cm pot, and their foliage will soon meld so that it appears like one mature specimen. In a shady corner of the patio or deck or by a shady doorway, they will make their attractive contribution for many months, and most will not collapse if you miss an occasional watering.

- *spring to fall foliage*
- *spring flowers*

*Robust but well-behaved perennial with invaluable color from spring to fall*

◀ The almost wholly silver foliage of 'Looking Glass' makes it one of the brightest of all foliage plants, and there are also the delightful blue spring flowers.

'Emerald Mist' features a bold and distinctive ring of bright silver marks around the middle of each heart-shaped leaf.

'Hadspen Cream' has leaves brightly edged in white. It is, however, noticeably less vigorous than most other varieties and has the unfortunate habit of reverting to plain green.

'Jack Frost' has foliage that is heavily silvered, but with a slim green rim around the edge of each leaf and a bright network of green veins.

'King's Ransom' has silver foliage and an attractive network of green veins while a gold band runs round the edge. This variety often scorches in dry conditions.

'Looking Glass' features foliage that is completely silver, with a green main vein through the center of the leaf and the most slender of green rims.

*Brunnera macrophylla*
Z3–8
14–18 × 18–24in
35–45 × 45–60cm

*Brunnera macrophylla* 'Emerald Mist'
Z3–8
14–18 × 18–24in
35–45 × 45–60cm

*Brunnera macrophylla* 'Hadspen Cream'
Z3–8
14–18 × 18–24in
35–45 × 45–60cm

*Brunnera macrophylla* 'Jack Frost'
Z3–8
14–18 × 18–24in
35–45 × 45–60cm

*Brunnera macrophylla* 'King's Ransom'
Z3–8
14–18 × 18–24in
35–45 × 45–60cm

*Brunnera macrophylla* 'Looking Glass'
Z3–8
14–18 × 18–24in
35–45 × 45–60cm

## ESSENTIALS

- All are good in shady borders with lacy ferns, shade-loving irises, and narrow-leaved hostas, perhaps with the addition of blushed pink impatiens. All also make good specimens for medium-sized containers in partial shade.

- Best in partial or full shade in any reasonable soil; all but 'Hadspen Cream' and 'King's Ransom' will also grow in dry shade and in full sun if the soil is kept moist.

- Cut back the ragged foliage before winter; snip out the fading flowers if time allows.

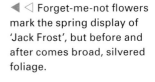

◀ ◁ Forget-me-not flowers mark the spring display of 'Jack Frost', but before and after comes broad, silvered foliage.

◁ ◀ 'King's Ransom' adds a variable creamy edge to the silvered leaves of 'Jack Frost'.

## *Buddleja*

# butterfly bush

**deciduous shrub**

- *spring to fall foliage*
- *summer and fall flowers*
- *attracts butterflies*

*A cascade of late-season flowers and striking foliage on easy, resilient shrubs*

Buddleias are grown for their fountain of flowering plumes in summer and fall, but the attractive foliage of a chosen few elevates them to genuine powerhouse status. Even amongst these, careful selection and sometimes observant care is necessary; most are forms of *B. davidii*, vigorous shrubs that start out relatively upright then arch over as the flowers open.

Variegated varieties spring first to mind, making an impact from early spring when the new leaves first start to stretch and display themselves. Avoid 'Variegata', which often produces green shoots that will soon dominate the shrub. A better choice is the gray-green foliage of 'Harlequin', a variegated form of the popular 'Royal Red'. The leaves have a yellow edge as they first open, fading to cream in summer, and make a colorful background to the reddish purple flower spikes. 'Harlequin' too may revert but less often than 'Variegata'. 'Florence' features both pale variegation and pale flowers.

'Masquerade' ('Notbud'),

also derived from 'Royal Red', is even more stable and the flowers are more reddish than 'Harlequin.' But the real pick is 'Santana', with irregular yellow margins becoming creamy relatively late in the summer and providing a bright contrast to the purple flower spikes.

In an altogether different style, 'Silver Anniversary' ('Morning Mist') features bright silver foliage, which may remain on the plant all winter in favored areas, and honey-scented white flowers in late summer and fall.

Buddleias are amongst the best of all garden shrubs to attract butterflies, moths, and hummingbirds (which feed on their nectar) and butterfly larvae (which feed on the foliage). But it's important to note that, in some areas, buddleias are considered invasive and planting them is not recommended. Heed local advice.

▶ A swallowtail butterfly feeds on the flowers of 'Harlequin', whose cream-edged gray-green foliage makes a striking display before and during flowering.

shoots to develop low on the plant, making better visual connections with low-growing neighbors, and plants will reach the lower end of the height guidance given here. Prune back to just 24in/60cm, and flowers will open on noticeably taller plants.

'Hint of Gold' ('Lisaura') is the most heat-tolerant of the yellow-leaved types, although the foliage becomes closer to chartreuse as it matures. 'Hint of Gold' also features broader leaves than others of this type and more upright growth.

'Lil Miss Sunshine' ('Janice')

## ESSENTIALS

- Choose plants that harmonize with the early foliage. Replicating the color of the later bloom works well, too, so blue columbines such as 'Roman Bronze' or even bright blue forget-me-nots suit yellow-leaved types and 'Sterling Silver'.

- Happiest in full sun in a fertile but well-drained soil. May be cut down to the ground in severe climates but often regrows.

- Prune hard as growth begins in spring, cutting down almost to ground level, to 6–9in/15–23cm or taller. Do not allow emerging growth to be overshadowed by larger neighbors.

◀ ◁ The foliage of 'Summer Sorbet' varies from having a neat yellow rim to all-yellow.

◁ ◀ The purplish stems and silver foliage of 'Sterling Silver' ('Lissilv') make an effective combination before the blue flowers open.

cloud—which makes a good back-of-the-border feature. In late spring the clusters of pale blue flowers are shown off beautifully.

More recently introduced and with longer, more slender foliage, 'Lemon and Lime' is a variegated version of the favorite 'Cynthia Postan' and has a more airy and refined look.

With a much lower, more spreading and mounding habit of growth are two variegated forms of *C. griseus*, 'Diamond Heights' and 'Silver Surprise'. With its deep green center and broad limey yellow edge, and its pale blue flowers in late spring and early summer,

'Diamond Heights' is ideal trailing over a sunny stone retaining wall.

'Silver Surprise' ('Brass') is in between 'Diamond Heights' and 'Pershore Zanzibar' in growth, making a broad mound, the edges of the dark green leaves marked in silvery white. The blue flowers appear in late spring.

Finally, for something completely different: 'Tuxedo' ('FIT02'), a black-leaved version of the old favorite 'Autumnal Blue'. Yes, black. Found in Ireland in 2007, it flowers mainly in summer and fall. Surprise!

*Ceanothus griseus* **'Diamond Heights'**
Z8–10
1 × 4ft
0.3 × 1.2m

*Ceanothus griseus* **'Silver Surprise' ('Brass')**
Z8–10
2–3 × 6–8ft
0.6–0.9 × 1.8–2.4m

*Ceanothus* **'Lemon and Lime'**
Z8–10
6–8 × 6–8ft
1.8–2.4 × 1.8–2.4m

*Ceanothus* **'Pershore Zanzibar' ('Zanzibar')**
Z8–10
6–8 × 4–6ft
1.8–2.4 × 1.2–1.8m

*Ceanothus* **'Tuxedo' ('FIT02')**
Z8–10
6–8 × 6–8ft
1.8–2.4 × 1.8–2.4m

## ESSENTIALS

• Often best planted against a wall, especially in areas where they are marginally hardy. Use as hosts for clematis or other lightweight climbers to create attractive combinations.

• Happy in full sun or a little shade, and any fertile but well-drained soil. In bright light, the yellow coloring of variegated types can swamp the green completely; in partial shade the green coloring may be more dominant.

• Spring-flowering types can be pruned after flowering, later-flowering types in spring. Plants sited against walls will need tying in to wires or trellises and watering as they establish themselves.

◀ The bright leaf edge of 'Pershore Zanzibar' ('Zanzibar') frames the blue flowers nicely but becomes greener by winter, especially when not in direct sun.

## *Cercis*

# redbud

**deciduous tree**

- *spring shoots and flowers*
- *summer foliage*
- *fall foliage color*

*Vivid spring display and spectacular fall color on an attractive small tree*

These intriguing members of the pea family begin the season by opening their clusters of flowers directly from last year's branches and even older branches—which can result in an unusually colorful tree. In shades of purple, magenta, pink, or white, the flowers often crowd the branches, making an impressive spring spectacle. In some, flowering is followed by purple foliage, then almost all develop lovely buttery autumn color and, often, attractive flat seedpods. Most of those grown belong to one of two species, one from North America and one from Europe.

From North America comes *C. canadensis* (eastern redbud), which makes a bushy tree and is ideal in smaller gardens. The clusters of vivid, purplish pink flowers line the branches prolifically in spring. Bronze-tinted new shoots follow and open to attractive heart-shaped leaves, 4in/10cm wide and long. Flowering much more reliably in its native land than in Britain, there are forms with flowers in various red and pink shades, plus white; 'Lavender Twist'

('Covey') features pink flowers held on slightly twisted, weeping branches. In the best variety, 'Forest Pansy', the leaves are dark reddish purple all summer. All forms turn bright buttery yellow in fall and develop 3in/7.5cm seedpods.

From Europe comes *C. siliquastrum*, the Judas tree—so called because it is said to be the tree from which Judas hanged himself. The flower clusters, in pink, deep purple, or white, are held at points where shoots divide and sometimes on the bare trunk. Occasionally used in salads, the flowers have an unusual sweet/acid flavor. Again, buttery fall color and larger pods, up to 5in/12.5cm long, complete the series of attractions. The Judas tree is familiar in Britain, especially in the south, where it flowers particularly well, but is usually displaced in American gardens by the native species.

▶ The rich purple foliage of 'Forest Pansy' may fade to a greener shade in hot conditions, but even that two-tone effect is delightful.

red veins), and 'White Moth' (creamy white).

Following them, the big and bright, large-flowered clematis are, with few exceptions, grown for their flowers alone; however, the honeyed seedheads of 'Duchess of Albany' and the yellowish fruits of 'Nelly Moser' are striking. Other large-flowered varieties known for their seedheads: 'Bees' Jubilee' (mauve pink, with a darker central bar), 'Blue Moon' ('Everin') (white, tinted lilac), 'Doctor Ruppel' (deep pink, with an even darker central bar), 'Gillian Blades' (creamy white with a hint of blue), 'H. F. Young' (blue), 'Lasurstern' (deep lavender blue), 'Miss Bateman' (pure white), 'Mrs Cholmondeley' (large, lavender blue flowers), and 'The President' (rich purple).

In summer and early autumn, the climbing orange-peel types (so called because of the color and texture of their petals)—*C. orientalis*, *C. tangutica*, *C. tibetana*, and their hybrids—feature heavy-textured, four-petalled flowers in orange and yellow shades over a long period and a second act of impressive seedheads, which begin in a slinky pewter shade maturing to fluffy silver. 'Bill McKenzie' is bright yellow with a reddish brown center and large seedheads; 'Golden Tiara' ('Kugotia') is less vigorous, with slightly orange-yellow dark-centered flowers that soon open flat. 'Lambton Park' has unusually large, bright yellow flowers with a green center and very large seedheads. 'Orange Peel' has golden yellow flowers opening from globular buds, becoming more orange as they mature.

Last amongst the climbing clematis: two large and very vigorous species are too overwhelming for many town gardens, but if they are given much more space in a rural situation, they can be spectacular—in flower and fruit. Both combine prolific flowering with a huge mass of late-season seedheads in the familiar style. The American *C. virginiana* has small gappy, cream-centered white flowers in late summer and autumn followed by bright silvery seedheads. The British *C. vitalba* has slightly duller flowers, but its seedheads regularly persist well into the winter, when they are popular with finches and good for drying for the house.

Two perennials, in their different ways, also feature. The short (in stature) but long-flowering *C. integrifolia* is a top plant, the flowers and silver seedheads overlapping for a few weeks, creating a

## ESSENTIALS

- Large-flowered types can be guided up a trellis or early-flowering shrubs; perennials can sprawl through low shrubs or stouter perennials, or can tumble over low walls. The vigorous climbers are ideal romping through mature conifers or apple trees.

- Both climbers and perennials are happy in full sun in any reasonable soil that is not waterlogged or parched; the climbers appreciate cool roots.

- Prune spring-flowering *C. alpina* and *C. macropetala* types and early-flowering large-flowered clematis after flowering; prune later-flowering large-flowered and orange-peel clematis as growth begins in spring. Cut perennials back hard in spring.

◀ After these lovely spring flowers are over, 'Jacqueline du Pré' produces a mass of silvery seedheads.

delightful combination in the midst of an extended season. 'Alba' has pure white flowers, 'Hendersonii' has unusually large, very dark blue flowers, and 'Rosea' has pink flowers.

Finally, a few forms of the perennial *C. recta* offer the singular beauty of purple coloring in their young foliage. 'Purpurea' is the most often seen, but 'Velvet Night' is a deeper, richer color. Both also feature loose heads of starry white flowers, which open in summer as the foliage is developing green tints.

*Clematis* **'Bees' Jubilee'**
Z4–9
6–8 × 2–3ft
1.8–2.4 × 0.6–0.9m

*Clematis* **'Bill McKenzie'**
Z4–9
13–16 × 4–5ft
4–5 × 1.2–1.5m

*Clematis* **'Blue Moon' ('Everin')**
Z4–9
6–8 × 2–3ft
1.8–2.4 × 0.6–0.9m

*Clematis* **'Columbine'**
Z6–9
6–10 × 4–5ft
1.8–3 × 1.2–1.5m

*Clematis* **'Constance'**
Z6–9
6–10 × 4–5ft
1.8–3 × 1.2–1.5m

*Clematis* **'Doctor Ruppel'**
Z4–9
6–8 × 2–3ft
1.8–2.4 × 0.6–0.9m

*Clematis* **'Duchess of Albany'**
Z4–9
6–8 × 2–3ft
1.8–2.4 × 0.6–0.9m

*Clematis* **'Fireworks'**
Z4–9
6–8 × 2–3ft
1.8–2.4 × 0.6–0.9m

*Clematis* **'Foxy'**
Z6–9
6–10 × 4–5ft
1.8–3 × 1.2–1.5m

**Clematis 'Frankie'**
Z6–9
6–10 × 4–5ft
1.8–3 × 1.2–1.5m

**Clematis 'Gillian Blades'**
Z4–9
6–8 × 2–3ft
1.8–2.4 × 0.6–0.9m

**Clematis 'Golden Tiara'**
**('Kugotia')**
Z5–9
8–10 × 5–7ft
2.4–3 × 1.5–2.1m

**Clematis 'H. F. Young'**
Z4–9
6–8 × 2–3ft
1.8–2.4 × 0.6–0.9m

**Clematis integrifolia**
Z3–7
20–24 × 20–24in
50–60 × 50–60cm

**Clematis integrifolia 'Alba'**
Z3–7
20–24 × 20–24in
50–60 × 50–60cm

**Clematis integrifolia**
**'Hendersonii'**
Z3–7
20–24 × 20–24in
50–60 × 50–60cm

**Clematis integrifolia 'Rosea'**
Z3–7
20–24 × 20–24in
50–60 × 50–60cm

**Clematis 'Jacqueline du Pré'**
Z6–9
6–10 × 4–5ft
1.8–3 × 1.2–1.5m

**Clematis 'Lambton Park'**
Z5–9
13–16 × 4–5ft
4–5 × 1.2–1.5m

◀ The shining silvered seed-heads follow purple blue flowers on *C. integrifolia*.

▲ 'Purpurea' wins fans with its purple-tinted young leaves and fragrant white flowers.

*Clematis* 'Lasurstern'
Z4–9
6–8 × 2–3ft
1.8–2.4 × 0.6–0.9m

*Clematis* 'Markham's Pink'
Z6–9
6–10 × 4–5ft
1.8–3 × 1.2–1.5m

*Clematis* 'Miss Bateman'
Z4–9
6–8 × 2–3ft
1.8–2.4 × 0.6–0.9m

*Clematis* 'Mrs Cholmondeley
Z4–9
6–8 × 2–3ft
1.8–2.4 × 0.6–0.9m

*Clematis* 'Nelly Moser'
Z4–9
6–8 × 2–3ft
1.8–2.4 × 0.6–0.9m

*Clematis* 'Orange Peel'
Z4–9
13–16 × 4–5ft
4–5 × 1.2–1.5m

*Clematis* 'Pink Flamingo'
Z6–9
6–10 × 4–5ft
1.8–3 × 1.2–1.5m

*Clematis recta* 'Purpurea'
Z3–7
3–6ft × 24–30in
0.9–1.8m × 60–75cm

*Clematis recta* 'Velvet Night'
Z3–7
3–6ft × 24–30in
0.9–1.8m × 60–75cm

*Clematis* 'The President'
Z4–9
6–8 × 2–3ft
1.8–2.4 × 0.6–0.9m

*Clematis virginiana*
Z3–8
20–25 × 6–10ft
6–7.5 × 1.8–3m

*Clematis vitalba*
Z4–9
20–30 × 8–12ft
6–9 × 2.4–3.5m

*Clematis* 'White Moth'
Z6–9
6–10 × 4–5ft
1.8–3 × 1.2–1.5m

▲ 'Gillian Blades' is one of the few large-flowered hybrids that go on to produce valuable seedheads.

# summersweet, sweet pepper bush

## Clethra

**deciduous shrub**

Adaptable shrubs, once their main requirements are met, clethras are best in acid soil and moist conditions, but they will flower well in shade, never grow too large for even the smallest of gardens, rarely need pruning, and provide two impressive features—three if you include the scent—at different seasons.

The plants tend to be well branched and upright, so low perennials will sneak right up to the stem. The dark foliage is rounded, sometimes wider towards the tip, then in late summer the flowers appear. The plumes, almost always in white and also held upright, have a sweet vanilla fragrance. The fall color following the

- *summer flowers*
- *fall foliage color*

*Fragrant, moisture-loving, late-flowering shrubs turn bright yellow in autumn*

◀ The scented pink flowers of 'Ruby Spice' are followed by a dramatic change as the leaves turn to buttery yellow in autumn.

## ESSENTIALS

- Use clethras as specimens in shade gardens or mixed borders that do not dry out in summer and as a refreshing change amongst rhododendrons in acid shade.

- Damp, acid soil is essential; clethras hate lime, and while they are not water plants, they will take wet soil for longer than most shrubs. Flowering well in shade, if moisture is consistent, they will also thrive in sun.

- No pruning is necessary; pests and diseases are rare.

◀ The fragrant white flowers of 'Hummingbird' are followed by buttery fall color.

flowers is simple: yellow, bright with few subtleties. The strings of seed capsules, maturing with the yellow leaves, while noticeable, could not be said to be more than interesting.

In recent years has come a flurry of new clethras that are distinct improvements on the dependable favorite, the wild *C. alnifolia*. 'Hummingbird',

the delightfully named 'Sixteen Candles', and 'Crystalina' are all short and almost mounded when mature. 'Vanilla Spice' is taller, with unusually large flowers. 'Ruby Spice' may not be ruby red, except in bud, but it is neater and a richer color than the old pale pink 'Rosea'; the more light it gets, the stronger its color.

*Clethra alnifolia*
Z3–9
8 × 8ft
2.4 × 2.4m

*Clethra alnifolia* 'Crystalina'
Z4–9
28–36 × 28–36in
70–90 × 70–90cm

*Clethra alnifolia* 'Hummingbird'
Z3–9
2–4 × 3–5ft
0.6–1.2 × 0.9–1.5m

*Clethra alnifolia* 'Rosea'
Z3–9
8 × 8ft
2.4 × 2.4m

*Clethra alnifolia* 'Ruby Spice'
Z4–8
4–6 × 3–5ft
1.2–1.8 × 0.9–1.5m

*Clethra alnifolia* 'Sixteen Candles'
Z4–9
4–5 × 2–3ft
1.2–1.5 × 0.6–0.9m

*Clethra alnifolia* 'Vanilla Spice'
Z4–9
3–6 × 3–5ft
0.9–1.8 × 0.9–1.5m

# conifers

**evergreen trees and shrubs** (occasionally deciduous)

- *spring shoots*
- *bark and cones*
- *fall foliage color*

*From the subtle to the startling, large and small, conifers have it all*

Conifers range from the towering sequoias of California to the tight and twiggy little junipers of the Arctic. Some, perhaps surprisingly, are deciduous; many have especially appealing new spring growth, patterned bark, or attractive cones. For discriminating gardeners, the most important will reveal a succession of foliage colors through the seasons. For the most part, these fall into three genera: false cypresses (*Chamaecyparis*), Japanese cedars (*Cryptomeria*), and arborvitae (*Thuja*). The tendency of the best of these varieties is to mature from golden or green summer foliage to bronze or copper or purplish foliage in winter; the four named here are slow growing, never overdominant

▶ ▷ A classic garden conifer for changing foliage, *Thuja occidentalis* 'Rheingold' is bright yellow in high summer and moves to coppery gold in winter.

▷ ▶ In autumn the foliage of *Metasequoia glyptostroboides*, one of a small number of deciduous conifers, turns from pink through gold to rusty brown.

## ESSENTIALS

- The uses of these conifers vary dramatically, from stately specimens as focal points in large gardens to neat domes for small raised beds or even containers. Check the mature heights carefully before buying, even as you remember that trees may take many decades to reach full size.

- Most appreciate full sun and fairly fertile soil that is not waterlogged, but check the conditions required by large trees in particular.

- Support larger trees well in their youth, and try to retain low branches to enhance their elegant shape. Few conifers regrow after pruning, but maturing specimens are usually improved by the removal of low branches if they become sparsely clothed with foliage.

in the garden, and the subtlety of their successional coloring is best appreciated at close quarters.

*Chamaecyparis thyoides* 'Ericoides' is compact and conical in shape, with soft blue-green summer foliage turning reddish brown to reddish violet in winter.

*Cryptomeria japonica* 'Vilmoriniana' grows slowly into a rounded ball of bright green summer foliage, maturing to reddish bronze in winter.

*Thuja occidentalis* 'Rheingold' is probably the star in this shifting sky, its soft and prettily divided, clean bright yellow summer foliage maturing to rich and subtle coppery tones in winter.

*Thuja orientalis* 'Rosedalis' makes a dense and rounded plant with soft foliage whose new spring growth is yellow, maturing to sea green in summer and then darkening to plum purple or brown-tinted in winter.

Many, much larger conifers featured in the broader landscape—firs, spruces, pines—have other attractions, including beautifully patterned and colored, slightly flaking bark. Cones, of course, can be large and impressive in some species and may be carried in generous quantities, lining the branches of cedars and firs.

Sometimes forgotten are the new spring shoots, which can be strikingly different from the mature foliage.

The silver firs are very stately trees and also some of those with the brightest foliage, as well as impressive purplish cones. *Abies koreana* (Korean fir) is probably the most popular, partly because of its relatively modest growth. Its needles are white underneath and in 'Silberlocke' rolled upwards to reveal their brightness; purple cones stand up from the branches. Nordmann's fir (*A. nordmanniana*), increasingly popular as a Christmas tree, reaches very impressive heights when mature; the tiered branches are dramatic, with shining green needles striped in white below, and the huge cones are up to 8in/20cm in length, maturing from green to violet blue, with pinkish orange lips peeping out.

Spruces include some of the most elegant of specimen trees with Brewer's weeping spruce, *Picea breweriana*, perhaps the most strikingly elegant of all and also featuring 4in/10cm green cones that mature to purple. The slender *P. omorika* (Serbian spruce) is a fine specimen with reddish cones and ideal for a tight corner. *Picea pungens* (Colorado spruce) is probably the best known, with many forms—including weeping, spreading, conical, and dwarf—featuring silvery gray blue leaves and pendulous cinnamon-colored cones up to 4in/10cm long.

Of the pines, *Pinus bungeana*, a fine specimen tree, offers the best bark, in flakes of white, gray, cream, yellow, amber, and purple; it shines particularly in the low winter sunlight. The Japanese red pine, *P. densiflora*, has reddish young bark maturing to a variety of russet and silver shades often shown off well by the development of multiple

trunks; in its popular variegated form, 'Oculus Draconis', the needles are striped in yellow. *Pinus pinea* (stone pine) becomes a very dramatic, widely spread tree as it matures; its huge cones yield the pine nuts used in cooking.

Finally, three widely grown conifers that are not only deciduous but feature bright fall color. The maidenhair tree, *Ginkgo biloba*, develops into a distinctively branched specimen tree with pretty, fresh green foliage like that of the maidenhair fern. In fall, the leaves turn the brightest clear

yellow. Variegated forms are also available, with the foliage streaked in cream or yellow, as well as weeping, dwarf, or slender upright varieties.

The swamp or bald cypress, *Taxodium distichum*, is a tall and narrow, moisture-loving tree from Florida's Everglades, with several valuable qualities. Its bark is reddish and fibrous, and it develops intriguing "knees," woody structures that emerge above ground from the roots below. The grassy, finely divided foliage is attractive all summer, then turns bronzy yellow in fall.

◀ The Japanese red pine, *Pinus densiflora*, is an impressive specimen where there is enough space. Its peeling bark, reddish new shoots, and cones are all valuable features.

▲ 'Oculus Draconis' is a slower growing form of *Pinus densiflora* with colorfully variegated foliage.

The similar dawn redwood, *Metasequoia glyptostroboides*, is tall and vigorous but narrowly conical in growth, its shaggy cinnamon brown bark striking all year. Finely divided, fresh green leaves turn first pinkish, then gold, and finally reddish brown in fall.

**Abies koreana**
Z5–6
30 × 20ft
9 × 6m

**Abies koreana 'Silberlocke'**
Z5–6
30 × 20ft
9 × 6m

**Abies nordmanniana**
Z4–6
130 × 20ft
40 × 6m

**Chamaecyparis thyoides 'Ericoides'**
Z5–8
4–6 × 2–3ft
1.2–1.8 × 0.6–0.9m

**Cryptomeria japonica 'Vilmoriniana'**
Z6–9
1–2 × 1–2ft
30–60 × 30–60cm

**Ginkgo biloba**
Z5–9
80–100 × 20–25ft
25–30 × 6–8m

**Metasequoia glyptostroboides**
Z5–10
70–130 × 12–15ft
21–40 × 3.5–4.5m

**Picea breweriana**
Z6–8
30–50 × 10–12ft
10–15 × 3–3.5m

**Picea omorika**
Z5–8
60–70 × 6–10ft
18–21 × 1.8–3m

**Picea pungens**
Z3–8
40–50 × 10–15ft
12–15 × 3–4.5m

**Pinus densiflora**
Z4–7
50–80 × 15–22ft
15–25 × 5–7m

**Pinus densiflora 'Oculus Draconis'**
Z4–7
40–60 × 40–60ft
12–18 × 12–18m

**Pinus pinea**
Z8–10
50–70 × 20–40ft
15–21 × 6–12m

**Taxodium distichum**
Z5–9
50–70 × 20–30ft
15–21 × 6–9m

**Thuja occidentalis 'Rheingold'**
Z2–7
3–5 × 3–5ft
0.9–1.5 × 0.9–1.5m

**Thuja orientalis 'Rosedalis'**
Z6–9
36 × 18in
90 × 45cm

# flowering dogwood     *Cornus*

**deciduous tree**

Two three-season stars, the American *C. florida* and the Asian *C. kousa*, are amongst the most colorful of all small trees. Their chief glories are their large and prolific, four-petalled spring flowers, in white or pink shades, and their fiery fall color. Most will also produce red fall fruits, much favored by wildlife, and the foliage of some is colorfully variegated; so most varieties will provide two seasons of distinct color and interest, and the truly spectacular ones will deliver four different features as the months roll by.

The fact that *C. florida* grows naturally from chilly

- *spring flowers*
- *fall foliage color and fruits*

*Valuable flowering and foliage trees, of manageable size and in many combinations*

◀ The Japanese dogwood, *C. kousa*, brings us prolific early summer flowers in pink or white followed by red, strawberry-like fruits.

87

- Flowering dogwoods are best carefully placed as specimen trees. Those grown for flowers and fall color can be planted where admiration is from a distance; the variegated types repay closer inspection.

- Both *C. kousa* and especially *C. florida* insist on neutral or acid soil, preferably also fertile but well drained and never becoming parched. They tend to develop into more elegant specimens with at least some shade, although this seems less noticeable in the cooler British summers. *Cornus florida* can be difficult to establish in Britain.

- No pruning is necessary, but watch *C. florida* for anthracnose, a fungus disease that starts with leaf spots but can kill the entire tree; *C. kousa* and most hybrids are resistant.

◀ The North American dogwood 'Appalachian Spring' develops this lovely reddish fall color.

▲ The variegated summer foliage of 'Rainbow' turns red and purple in fall.

Massachusetts to balmy Florida and Mexico is encouraging for the gardener, and the wild species itself is a very attractive tree. Unfortunately, the climate in Britain and the Pacific Northwest suits this species less well. Disease-resistant and large-flowered 'Appalachian Spring' is the pick, with an excellent fall show, and two variegated forms stand out for their color and their reliability. The foliage of the rather upright 'Rainbow' is edged in yellow, the margins turning orange and then red, the center red then purple; 'Firebird' is similar but makes a more rounded tree.

The disease-resistant Chinese dogwood, *C. kousa*, features a similar double appeal of white to red spring flowers and rich fall color; 'Milky Way' also has unusually large edible fruits. Amongst the fewer variegated forms of this species, 'Gold Star' and 'Samaritan' ('Samzan') stand out.

These two species have been crossed to create disease-resistant hybrids that are often prolific in bloom. 'Celestial' ('Rutdan') is vigorous and large-flowered, with a green tint to its white flowers and resistance to the main dogwood pest, dogwood borer; 'Celestial Shadow' is a variegated form of 'Celestial' with yellow-edged leaves turning deep plum with reddish edges in fall. 'Venus' ('KN-30-8'), with a slightly different background, is vigorous, very large-flowered, and unusually quick-growing.

*Cornus* 'Celestial' ('Rutdan')
Z5–9
14–18 × 12–15ft
4–5.5 × 3.5–4.5m

*Cornus* 'Celestial Shadow'
Z5–9
10–12 × 8–10ft
3–3.5 × 2.4–3m

*Cornus florida*
Z5–8
20 × 25ft
6 × 8m

*Cornus florida* 'Appalachian Spring'
Z5–8
10 × 6ft
3 × 1.8m

*Cornus florida* 'Firebird'
Z5–8
15–18 × 15–18ft
4.5–5.5 × 4.5–5.5m

*Cornus florida* 'Rainbow'
Z5–8
10 × 8ft
3 × 2.4m

*Cornus kousa*
Z5–8
22 × 15ft
7 × 4.5m

*Cornus kousa* 'Gold Star'
Z5–8
8 × 6ft
2.4 × 1.8m

*Cornus kousa* 'Milky Way'
Z5–8
22 × 15ft
7 × 4.5m

*Cornus kousa* 'Samaritan' ('Samzan')
Z5–9
20 × 15ft
6 × 4.5m

*Cornus* 'Venus' ('KN-30-8')
Z5–9
8–10 × 10–12ft
2.4–3 × 3–3.5m

# redtwig dogwood

**Cornus**

**deciduous shrub**

These invaluable shrubs all feature bright and colorful winter stems, white spring flowers, lovely fall leaf color, and autumn berries. Three species from around the world are involved here—*C. alba* from Asia, *C. sanguinea* from Europe, and *C. sericea* from North America—and each offers an outstanding variety, especially for small spaces.

*Cornus alba* 'Spaethii', one of the finest variegated shrubs, has pink spring leaf shoots and glossy golden-edged leaves from spring to fall, when the leaves turn plummy and pink; its red stems shine in winter. *Cornus sanguinea* 'Winter

- *winter stems*
- *spring flowers*
- *fall foliage color and fruits*

*Year-round treasures, with colorful winter stems plus floral and foliar appeal*

◀ An essential dogwood, 'Winter Beauty' features red-tipped pale amber winter twigs and buttery yellow fall foliage color.

91

Beauty' features yellow stems, the color drifting into orange-red at the shoot tips, while the green leaves turn yellow in fall. The vigorous *C. sericea* 'Flaviramea' has bright, greenish yellow winter stems following yellow and orange fall color.

With many other redtwig dogwoods from which to choose, a quick summary of the rest of the best seems appropriate. Between them they offer an outstanding range of colors right through the year.

## ESSENTIALS

- Redtwig dogwoods are lovely underplanted with dwarf blue bulbs like scillas and chionodoxa, or with snowdrops. Set varieties of viticella clematis to scramble through and flower in summer.

- Happy in any reasonable soils, including those which are consistently damp. The best stem color is produced in full sun.

- Pruning hard, almost to ground level, every spring, is essential to promote the best stem color.

◀ ◁ The vertical red stems of the easy-to-grow 'Sibirica' bring months of valuable bright winter color.

◁ ◀ Variegated forms such as 'Hedgerows Gold' develop rich autumnal shades to follow their summer variegation.

## ESSENTIALS

- While *C. bullatus* is a fine boundary specimen, and stout enough to host a climber, *C. atropurpureus* and *C. horizontalis* are lovely arching over a low wall or against a north-facing fence, perhaps intermingled with winter jasmine, *Jasminum nudiflorum*.

- These cotoneasters are happy in good light and in most soils that are not waterlogged; fruiting is usually most prolific in full sun. Most tolerate drought once established.

- Little care needed except occasional pruning to improve the shape. Can be susceptible to woolly aphids, fireblight, and webber caterpillars.

◀ The white-edged leaves of 'Variegatus' develop reddish and orange shades in autumn, before falling to reveal the herringbone pattern of branches.

*Cotoneaster atropurpureus*
  **'Variegatus'**
  Z5–8
  18 × 26in
  45 × 65cm

*Cotoneaster bullatus*
  Z5–9
  12 × 10ft
  3.5 × 3m

*Cotoneaster horizontalis*
  Z5–8
  3 × 5ft
  0.9 × 1.5m

▲ The red berries of *C. horizontalis* follow pinkish spring flowers.

# evergreen cotoneaster

**evergreen shrub**

- *evergreen foliage*
- *spring flowers*
- *fall fruits*

*Commanding presence allied with bold foliage, spring flowers, and fall fruits*

These include some of the most dramatic of cotoneasters, developing into impressive specimen plants. The branches of taller types can be weighed down by the fruits which, as they soften over winter, increasingly sustain berry-eating birds. 'Cornubia', a selection of *C. frigidus*, is a stupendous plant, often developing into a small tree, with unusually large fruits in crowded clusters following showy white flowers. Two hybrids are likewise imposing choices; 'John Waterer' flowers and fruits prolifically, with clusters of white flowers and then glossy red fruits carried on arching shoots, and 'Rothschildianus' makes an elegant arching

▶ ▷ *Cotoneaster conspicuus*, a ground-covering type, presents the classic combination of white spring flowers and prolific red autumn berries on a vigorous mound-forming plant with arching branches.

▷ ▶ 'John Waterer' makes an impressive tall shrub dripping with autumn berries after white summer flowers.

## ESSENTIALS

- Other shade-loving early spring flowerers go well with *C. coum* (hellebores, dainty *Crocus tommassinianus*, blue scillas, chionodoxas), as does the emerging foliage of peonies. Then later, when cyclamen foliage is at its peak, not only does it help brighten dark places and hide the fading foliage of dwarf bulbs, but it also creates beguiling partnerships with later plants.

- Both species appreciate some shade cast by deciduous trees, summer-flowering perennials, or a fence or wall. Humus-rich, well-drained soil is ideal.

- Neither species needs much care, except for the removal of fading foliage when the time comes. After planting, simply leave them alone, and if conditions are good they should self-sow.

dainty flowers with backswept petals to shady situations.

Of the twenty species that can be found in catalogs, two stand out not only for their robust growth in the garden and their sparkling colors, but also for the fact that they are far more widely available than the other species.

Winter- and spring-flowering *C. coum* has dainty blooms in shades from magenta through pinks to white, with some uncommon but very appealing bicolors. It's a classic partner for other early shade lovers. The neat, rounded, slightly leathery leaves follow the flowers, overlapping late in the flowering season, and last all summer, bringing welcome light to shady places. In some, the foliage is dull green and not very interesting; in others, the foliage is bright silver or pewter in color or patterned in green and silver—these are the ones to look for.

**Cyclamen coum**
    Z5–9
    2–4 × 4–6in
    5–10 × 10–15cm

Flowering in late summer and fall with foliage gleaming through the winter and into spring, *C. hederifolium* is the most widely grown and the most varied in its foliage patterning. The flowers come in various pinks and white, occasionally scented, while the arrowhead-shaped leaves vary enormously in color and patterning. It's a matter of taste. I like those with entirely silvered leaves, and those with very clear and distinct markings. If you buy two different forms, you will soon have a range of patterns as they self-sow.

If buying by mail order, try to find named forms, as these are more likely to be dependably good; unnamed forms may be unpredictable in their coloring. When visiting a nursery, simply pick the colors and patterns you like best.

**Cyclamen hederifolium**
    Z6–9
    4–6 × 6–10in
    10–15 × 15–25cm

◀ *Cyclamen hederifolium* flowers in late summer and fall and also features silvered foliage over a long period.

# dahlia

**annual or half-hardy perennial**

- *spring to fall foliage*
- *summer and fall flowers*

*In the best forms, bright and colorful flowers are set off by sultry foliage*

Most dahlias are one-season wonders. But those with dark foliage contribute rare coloring from the day they are planted until the frosts of fall end their season. Some have glossy foliage that shines in the sun, while others lack that sheen; and leaves too vary in their shape, with some being sharply divided and with bright toothed edges to add to their appeal. This richness of foliage sets off the flowers beautifully. In general, dark-leaved dahlias tend to feature flowers, single or double, in bold or dark shades with very few pastel colors. But these combinations fit in well with other plants that help create tropical-style summer plantings.

The varieties in the Happy Single series are especially valuable as not only is their foliage rich and dark and their flowering prolific and in beautiful colors and color combinations, but the plants stay smaller than those of most dahlias, so they are ideal in containers and smaller gardens. The members of the Dark Angel series make even smaller plants, with jaggedly toothed leaves.

There are also some very impressive individual varieties, including 'Bishop of Llandaff' (vivid, dark red flowers set against toothed, blackish bronze leaves), 'David Howard' (coppery orange double flowers, bronzed green foliage), 'Ellen Houston' (vibrant orange-red double flowers, glossy bronze leaves), 'Fascination' (startling semi-double pink flowers, green-tinted bronze leaves), 'Knockout' (sharp yellow single flowers gleaming against almost black foliage), 'Magenta Star' (large, magenta pink single flowers, almost black leaves), and 'Twyning's After Eight' (white single flowers, with a faint blush on the back, against leaves the color of dark bitter chocolate).

▶ The double orange flowers of 'David Howard' stand out well against the mass of bronzed foliage.

have a cream or yellow edge to the leaf, some have a cream or yellow center. 'Astrid' has a narrow yellow edge that pales to cream, while 'G. K. Argles' is more vigorous, with margins edged in richer yellow and with larger flowers. 'Carol Mackie' also has yellow-edged leaves, turning cream, and is more dependable and hardier than most other forms. 'Briggs Moonlight' has a cream center to each leaf with only a narrow dark green edge and is dramatic but rather slow, while 'Golden Treasure' is similar but richer yellow in color.

*Daphne odora* includes the most popular of all variegated daphnes, 'Aureomarginata', with its narrow cream edges to the leaves combined with free flowering habit and unusual hardiness. The actual variegation is hardly noticeable from a distance. By contrast, 'Maejima' has a bright yellow edge to the leaf, set off by a dark green center.

*Daphne ×burkwoodii* 'Astrid'
Z5–8
3–5 × 3–5ft
0.9–1.5 × 0.9–1.5m

*Daphne ×burkwoodii* 'Briggs Moonlight'
Z5–8
24–30 × 18–24in
60–75 × 45–60cm

*Daphne ×burkwoodii* 'Carol Mackie'
Z5–8
36–40in × 3–5ft
90–100cm × 0.9–1.5m

*Daphne ×burkwoodii* 'G. K. Argles'
Z5–8
5–6 × 4–5ft
1.5–1.8 × 1.2–1.5m

*Daphne ×burkwoodii* 'Golden Treasure'
Z5–8
30–36 × 30–36in
75–90 × 75–90cm

*Daphne odora* 'Aureo-marginata'
Z7–9
4 × 4ft
1.2 × 1.2m

*Daphne odora* 'Mae-jima'
Z7–9
40–48 × 40–48in
1–1.2 × 1–1.2m

## ESSENTIALS

- Often best against a wall in a sheltered garden, protected from the coldest weather and where the floral fragrance is contained.

- Any reasonable soil that is not wet in winter is suitable; summer moisture ensures continuing growth and flowering. *Daphne odora* dislikes limy soils.

- Cut back any unusually vigorous shoots to create elegantly rounded plants.

◀ 'Mae-jima' is covered in these dramatic leaves year-round, while in winter and spring the clusters of fragrant flowers add to the display.

## Darmera

# umbrella plant, Indian rhubarb

**perennial**

- *spring flowers*
- *summer foliage*
- *fall foliage color*

*Impressive spring and summer acts are followed by sumptuous fall color*

Before any sign of the foliage, the flowers of this bold, moisture-loving perennial burst through the soil and into bloom. The slightly dome-shaped heads—carried on hairy, bare, slender but stout, slightly wavy or curved, reddish stems—are filled with blushed white to vivid pink florets, each with a dark pink center. As the flowers fade, the foliage surges through and hides the dying flower-heads. Each round but lobed leaf can grow to 24in/60cm across with the stem attached in the middle—hence the common name—but it's rather an upside-down umbrella that often holds the rain; the entire summer is marked by their bold presence. Then, as the days shorten in the autumn, the foliage turns shades of deep red, bringing a whole new range of rich tones to the plant.

A North American west coast native, *D. peltata* (formerly *Peltiphyllum peltatum*) is a moisture-loving perennial and, while it thrives along the margins of pools, ponds, and streams, where the plant will mature to its full height and its leaves mature to their full size, it will also thrive in moisture-retentive soil away from water, although in such situations it rarely develops its full glory.

The dwarf form 'Nana', whose foliage is half the usual width, is generally reckoned to be less hardy.

*Darmera peltata*
Z5–9
3–5 × 2–4ft
0.9–1.5 × 0.6–1.2m

*Darmera peltata* 'Nana'
Z7–8
12 × 12in
30 × 30cm

▶ As the season rolls to a close, the foliage of *D. peltata* takes a colorful turn and signs off with this coral red, or sometimes burgundy, tone.

## ESSENTIALS

- Lovely in shade gardens with other spring flowers, including yellow-leaved grasses and sedges, the bold foliage of hellebores, and the broad leaves of hostas.

- Best in dappled shade with consistently moist, but not waterlogged, humus-rich soil.

- Best deadheaded to avoid the spread of unwanted inferior seedlings. Tidy up the dead growth at the end of the season; divide and replant if the center of the plants becomes sparse.

◀ The finely cut foliage of 'Candy Hearts' opens silvery blue then greens a little and in spring is topped with a mass of pink lockets opening from dark buds.

▶ Some of the best of recent dicentras, like 'King of Hearts', feature unusually silvery blue foliage.

*Dicentra formosa* **'Bacchanal'**
Z3–9
18 × 24in
45 × 60cm

*Dicentra formosa* **'Langtrees'**
Z4–8
12 × 18in
30 × 45cm

*Dicentra formosa* **'Snowflakes'** **('Fusd')**
Z3–8
10 × 20in
25 × 50cm

*Dicentra* **'Ivory Hearts'**
Z3–8
9–12 × 9–12in
23–30 × 23–30cm

*Dicentra* **'King of Hearts'**
Z3–8
9–12 × 9–12in
23–30 × 23–30cm

*Dicentra peregrina*
Z3–8
4–6 × 6–9in
10–15 × 15–23cm

*Dicentra* **'Stuart Boothman'**
Z3–9
12 × 16in
30 × 40cm

## *Diphylleia*

# umbrellaleaf

**perennial**

- *spring shoots and flowers*
- *summer fruits*

*A bold, elegant, softly colorful woodlander with unusual multi-season appeal*

Related to *Podophyllum* and native to six southeastern U.S. states, *D. cymosa* attracts admiration, or at least interest, from the first signs of its emergence until late summer. The glossy, bronze-tinted foliage emerges in spring wrapped appealingly around the fat stems, looking like little hunched hermits, then expands until the two leaves are held at the top of the stems. Each broad leaf may extend to 18in/45cm across and resembles a jagged version of the more familiar *Darmera peltata*. In late spring clusters of white flowers open on long stems from the joint between the two leaves, and as summer progresses these give way to bright blue-purple berries,

like dainty little grapes—if the chipmunks and slugs ignore them as they ripen. To be fair, by this stage dry conditions or high temperatures may have set the foliage on a downward decline—it becomes yellow and ragged when stressed, often disappearing altogether. But this is a small price to pay for the preceding elements of interest.

Two very similar Asian species are occasionally seen: *D. grayi* and *D. sinensis* both have smaller leaves, redder stems, and berries in a more purplish shade. All are (admittedly unlikely) members of the barberry family and share the relative resistance to deer browsing that seems to be a family trait.

*Diphylleia cymosa*
Z7–10
36 × 18in
90 × 45cm

*Diphylleia grayi*
Z4–9
12–24 × 12–20in
30–60 × 30–50cm

*Diphylleia sinensis*
Z5–8
36 × 20in
90 × 50cm

▶ The large rounded foliage of the shade-loving *D. cymosa*, with its reddish patina, sets off clusters of white spring flowers.

spring there are clusters of violet flowers, and after the flowers a fresh flush of pink leaves emerges. Quite a stunner.

*Epimedium ×perralchicum* 'Fröhnleiten' is an evergreen with vivid young leaves in dark shrimp pink with green veins followed by yellow flowers.

Good ground cover and drought tolerant once established.

*Epimedium pinnatum* subsp. *colchicum* 'Thunderbolt' is an improved form of an old favorite, a very vigorous evergreen with bright yellow spring flowers and foliage turning blackish purple with the cool nights

## ESSENTIALS

- Lovely in shade gardens with other spring perennials, epimediums are best placed towards the front, where their intriguing flower structure and coloring can best be admired. Evergreens in particular make effective ground cover.

- Happiest in dappled or partial shade in moist, humus-rich soil, although the evergreens will take drier conditions and more sun when established.

- Water and feed in their first year to ensure plants settle in well. Cut back all the old foliage in late winter to best show off the new spring foliage and flowers.

◀ ◁ The new foliage of 'Fire Dragon' is a fine background for the bicolor flowers.

◁ ◀ This early foliage of 'Chocolate Lace' is followed by large creamy yellow flowers.

of autumn, often with a green forked lightning flash.

*Epimedium ×rubrum* is an evergreen hybrid bringing together the larger flowers of *E. grandiflorum* and the robustness of *E. alpinum* in a plant with reddish new foliage, reddish brown fall foliage, and crimson and yellow flowers in between.

*Epimedium ×versicolor*

'Neosulphureum' is evergreen with bronzed spring foliage and yellow flowers; the tough and weed-smothering 'Sulphureum' is also evergreen with coppery foliage and pale yellow flowers.

*Epimedium ×youngianum* 'After Midnight' has a brownish red edge to its new leaves, turning chocolate brown by the time the white flowers are set against them; 'Merlin' has coppery young leaves and rosy mauve flowers; 'Milk Chocolate' has small chocolate spring foliage speckled in green and lasts as backdrop to the display of white flowers; 'Niveum' has coppery young leaves and white flowers. All are deciduous.

**Epimedium alpinum**
Z4–9
14 × 12in
35 × 30cm

**Epimedium 'Black Sea'**
Z5–8
12–14 × 18–20in
30–35 × 45–50cm

**Epimedium 'Fire Dragon'**
Z5–8
12–14 × 20–24in
30–35 × 50–60cm

**Epimedium grandiflorum 'Chocolate Lace'**
Z5–8
10–12 × 12–14in
25–30 × 30–35cm

**Epimedium grandiflorum 'Dark Beauty'**
Z5–8
10–12 × 12–14in
25–30 × 30–35cm

**Epimedium grandiflorum 'Lilafee'**
Z5–8
10–12 × 10–12in
25–30 × 25–30cm

*Epimedium grandiflorum*
  'Queen Esta'
    Z5–8
    12–14 × 12–14in
    30–35 × 30–35cm

*Epimedium grandiflorum* 'Rose
  Queen'
    Z5–8
    18 × 15in
    45 × 38cm

*Epimedium* 'Lilac Cascade'
    Z5–8
    10–12 × 10–12in
    25–30 × 25–30cm

*Epimedium ×perralchicum*
  'Fröhnleiten'
    Z5–9
    16 × 24in
    40 × 60cm

*Epimedium pinnatum* subsp.
  *colchicum* 'Thunderbolt'
    Z5–9
    10–14 × 20–24in
    25–35 × 50–60cm

*Epimedium ×rubrum*
    Z4–8
    12 × 12in
    30 × 30cm

*Epimedium ×versicolor*
  'Neosulphureum'
    Z5–9
    12 × 12in
    30 × 30cm

*Epimedium ×versicolor*
  'Sulphureum'
    Z5–9
    14–16 × 18–20in
    35–40 × 45–50cm

*Epimedium ×youngianum*
  'After Midnight'
    Z6–9
    12 × 12–14in
    30 × 30–35cm

◀ Beautifully patterned new foliage opens above older, over-wintering leaves on 'Fröhnleiten'. The spring flowers are bright yellow.

▲ The new foliage of 'Milk Chocolate' is exactly that shade, and lasts to show off the white flowers beautifully.

purplish blue, so creating a whole new look at the stage when the flowers are little more than buds.

Their foliage too, can make a valuable feature. From the distinctive gray-blue, holly-like mounds of the British native *E. maritimum*, to the long, bluish, sword-like blades of the American *E. yuccifolium* to the prettily patterned *E. planum* and *E. variifolium*, they bring months of off-season color. Species from the Americas tend to be evergreen; those from Europe tend to be deciduous.

While the foliage of some is strikingly veined in white or cream, *E. planum* 'Jade Frost' is at present the only truly variegated form. Its leaves are

edged in pink as they unroll, maturing with a bright creamy white margin; the effect of the variegated rosette is dramatic, especially as the coloring is later carried right into the flowerhead.

The biennial *E. giganteum* is a little different. Often known as Miss Willmott's ghost—the 19th-century British gardener used to throw seeds in gardens she visited and the plants flowered much later, as ghosts of her visit. It overwinters as a bold rosette of glossy green, heart-shaped leaves up to 6in/15cm long; then, in summer, branched heads of silver flowers are surrounded by a jaggedly toothed silver ruff. Impressive.

## ESSENTIALS

- Most are striking over a gravel mulch, or integrated with other perennials. The taller American species make fine specimens.

- All insist on plenty of sunshine, and enjoy soil that is neither too rich nor too wet in winter. They are tolerant of dry conditions once established, and many are unexpectedly hardy.

- Taller types need discreet staking using short bamboo canes, while smaller, multibranched types are better supported with twigs.

*Eryngium alpinum*
  Z5–8
  28 × 18in
  70 × 45cm

*Eryngium bourgatii*
  Z5–9
  6–18 × 12in
  15–45 × 30cm

*Eryngium giganteum*
  Z6–9
  15–48 × 12–18in
  38–120 × 30–45cm

*Eryngium maritimum*
  Z5–10
  12–15 × 15–18in
  30–38 × 38–45cm

*Eryngium ×oliverianum*
  Z5–8
  36 × 18in
  90 × 45cm

*Eryngium planum*
  Z5–9
  12–36 × 12–18in
  30–90 × 30–45cm

*Eryngium planum* 'Jade Frost'
  Z5–9
  12–36 × 12–18in
  30–90 × 30–45cm

*Eryngium variifolium*
  Z5–9
  12–18 × 10–12in
  30–45 × 25–30cm

*Eryngium yuccifolium*
  Z4–9
  4–6 × 2–3ft
  1.2–1.8 × 0.6–0.9m

◀ The silvery thistles of *E. giganteum* follow a striking overwintering rosette of glossy heart-shaped leaves.

*Euphorbia*

# perennial spurge

**deciduous perennial**

- *spring shoots*
- *spring or summer flowers*
- *spring and summer foliage*

*Colorful shoots, foliage, and flowers in a shifting range of appealing combinations*

Euphorbias come in a variety of styles—from annual weeds to cactus-like succulents to the holiday poinsettia—and even considering only those best suited to mixed and perennial borders, the selection is impressive. Amongst the range of traditional perennials are some fine plants, but one in particular stands out—*E. polychroma* 'Bonfire'. It should be in every garden. From spring to fall, the tight and compact 'Bonfire' seems to be in constant flux: the shoots emerge green in spring, quickly becoming orange or purplish; the yellow flowers open; all summer the plant develops reddish or purplish tints, becoming fiery in fall. The precise tone of the coloring seems to depend on temperature and moisture, but this is one plant that is never, ever dull.

Also excellent is *E. polychroma* 'Candy' (formerly 'Purpurea'), whose shoots open purple, cradle vivid yellow flowers, and then turn green; the flowers too often show orange or pinkish tints.

In fact, all forms of the species are worth growing, and the botanical epithet gives a clue as to why—*polychroma* means "many colors," specifically describing the color change in the flowerheads as they mature. Most also feature fall foliage color, often pink or purplish, especially when grown in plenty of sun.

Perennial species from Asia offer a variation on the opening act. The slender vertical shoots of *E. donii*, *E. schillingii*, *E. sikkimensis*, and *E. wallichii* emerge in spring infused with strong pink or red coloring and a contrasting white stripe through the center of each young leaf; they can even appear braided. As the foliage matures, it loses some of the red tones but is re-enlivened in summer, when plants are topped with bold yellow flowerheads.

▶ The first green shoots of 'Bonfire' soon develop delightful purplish tints, against which the bright yellow flowerheads stand out.

- All are ideal in gravel gardens with dwarf bulbs, rosemary, thyme, and self-sown poppies. The lower silvery types are good with bronze sedges, libertias, and blue fescues.

- Happy in full sun with good drainage. The taller types are best sheltered from strong winds, while the showrter variegated ones are ideal in containers.

- As the flowers fade, the whole flowering shoot should be cut right out to allow space for the colorful new growth from the base to develop.

◄ The grayish evergreen foliage of 'Glacier Blue' is narrowly edged in pale cream all year round, and when the flowerheads stretch in late winter and spring, the variegation continues into the flowers.

▲ The vivid new growth of 'Red Wing' ('Charam') opens to chartreuse flowers and matures to purplish green.

*Euphorbia characacias* 'Glacier Blue'
Z7–9
18 × 18in
45 × 45cm

*Euphorbia characacias* 'Portuguese Velvet'
Z7–10
2 × 2ft
60 × 60cm

*Euphorbia characacias* 'Silver Swan' ('Wilcott')
Z7–9
3 × 4ft
0.9 × 1.2m

*Euphorbia characacias* 'Tasmanian Tiger'
Z7–9
15 × 18in
20 × 45cm

*Euphorbia characacias* subsp. *wulfenii* 'Lambrook Gold'
Z7–10
6 × 5ft
1.8 × 1.5m

*Euphorbia myrsinites*
Z5–8
4 × 15in
10 × 38cm

*Euphorbia* 'Red Wing' ('Charam')
Z6–10
20 × 20in
50 × 50cm

*Euphorbia rigida*
Z7–10
18 × 24in
45 × 60cm

▲ The snaky shoots of *E. myrsinites* are clad with silvery evergreen blue leaves with spring heads of chartreuse flowers at the tips.

# ferns

**perennial**

Impressive in their own right, lacy ferns are also perfect partners for many other shade-loving perennials, providing a welcome and surprising succession of color and fascination considering that they have no flowers at all. Firstly, in spring and occasionally until summer, the excitement begins as the new fronds start to unfurl. As the divisions in the fronds unroll, some quickly mature to fresh clear

- *unfurling fronds*
- *spring to fall foliage*
- *spores*

*Classic four-season perennials, with both subtlety and panache*

◀ *Athyrium* 'Burgundy Lace' goes through an astonishing transformation in color, from bright reddish purple in spring to a more subtle silver with red veins in summer.

- Good counterparts
  for hostas, bergenias,
  and other broad-leaved
  perennials; many athy-
  riums are also good in
  containers. Do not mask
  new spring growth with
  nearby plants.

- Most enjoy moist,
  humus-rich soil in at
  least partial shade;
  osmundas prefer plenty
  of moisture.

- Tidy away old fronds
  and mulch to retain
  moisture; there are
  few pest and disease
  problems.

◀ With red stems and creamy early coloring, *Athyrium otophorum* matures into pale green fronds with red veins.

▲ Early red croziers of *Athyrium filix-femina* 'Lady in Red' give way to a surge of red-stemmed spring growth with carries the familiar prettily divided foliage.

# forsythia

**deciduous shrub**

- *winter and spring flowers*
- *spring to fall foliage*

*Classic early flower color, now supplemented by colorful or variegated foliage*

Forsythias are plants of extremes. In winter and spring they are the brightest flowers in the garden; after flowering they are the most boring—and must serve as host to a late-flowering clematis or other climber in order to provide any color at all. Except . . . There are a few varieties with variegated foliage to continue color right through the season, and even a few with rich purple fall color. None, unfortunately, are widely available; I provide six from which to choose.

'Fiesta' brings a bright yellow zone, with a red midrib, to the center of each leaf, held on the plant longer in fall than with other variegated forsythias. The bright yellow flowers are held on red stems. Derived from 'Minigold' ('Flojor'), with the same compact habit and upright growth.

'Golden Times' is also prolific in flowering, with noticeably toothed yellow leaves that usually, though not always, have a green streak through the center. May scorch in bright sun if the soil is dry.

'Kumson' has its variegation in a different style, with leaf veins picked out in palest yellow or white. This is a dwarf form, which flowers well if not dramatically, and whose foliage is more intriguing, more subtle.

'New Hampshire Gold' features a real punch of early flowers; then, after a summer of green foliage, the leaves reliably turn reddish purple.

'Susan Gruninger' is a form of an old favorite, the large-flowered and prolific 'Lynwood', but with the addition of creamy white margins to the leaves. Unlike some marginal variegations, they do not crisp in the sun.

'Taff's Arnold', a selection of *F. suspensa* with lax growth and good flowers, features an unpredictable splashing of yellow on the leaves. The surprising bonus of purple fall foliage color can also be effective.

▶ The dwarf 'Kumson' sports the usual yellow flowers, but they are followed by these uniquely cream-veined leaves held on reddish stems, creating a delightful pattern all summer.

plants. But in many areas, fuchsias are grown exclusively as indoor plants or, preferably, as plants for summer containers; these tend to be large flowered, with broad fleshy foliage and dramatic variegations. Four are choice.

'Autumnale' is a trailer whose foliage opens in green and coppery tones then becomes more gold, and even purplish and red, depending on the light conditions. Purple and red flowers open in late summer.

'Golden Marinka' is a trailer with an unpredictable patterning of green and yellow foliage, with some all-yellow leaves. The flowers are rich red.

'John Ridding' ('Firecracker') is a strongly upright variegated form of the popular 'Thalia', with vivid pink shoot tips, gray-green leaves edged in white with pink tints, and clusters of long, slim orangered flowers. Ideal as a container centerpiece.

'Tom West' is a bushy trailer with pink shoots tips and graygreen leaves edged in pink on the younger shoots, maturing to a white edge, and enhanced by pink leaf stalks and midribs. The summer and early fall flowers are red and purple.

Hardier types are all forms of *F. magellanica*; these have even become naturalized in Ireland, California, and Oregon, where they form longlasting hedges. Often their top growth is knocked back in winter, and they regrow from ground level. The foliage is a little longer and narrower than container types, less solid in texture, with more slender flowers. Again, there are four fine variegated forms, some with pink shoots tips, all of which flower for many weeks and may carry reddish purple edible fruits. 'Sharpitor' has cream- or yellow-edged leaves and blushed white flowers; 'Tricolor' has creamy variegation and red and purple flowers; 'Variegata' has foliage with a broad white edge and slender red flowers; and 'Versicolor' has grayish leaves, pink-tinted when young, with a narrow white edge and slender red flowers.

## ESSENTIALS

- Large-flowered, less hardy fuchsias are ideal in tubs and baskets with summer annuals. Smaller-flowered, hardier types are good in mixed borders.

- In summer grow in full sun in cool climates, shade in hot climates; keep moist but not soggy. In cool mild areas, grow hardier types in full sun.

- Pinch out container types when young to encourage bushy growth; overwinter in frost-free conditions. Prune outdoor types in spring, cutting back to sturdy growth or cutting off frost-damaged shoots.

◀ The aptly named 'Autumnale' ranges through these attractive foliar tones and also carries red and purple flowers on its trailing shoots.

flowers add new short-season sparks to a long season of foliage color.

*Geranium* 'Ann Folkard' has foliage which emerges in a golden yellow mound then the extensive (non-rooting) trailing shoots set their black-veined magenta flowers against smaller yellow leaves. Good ground cover that will even climb into mature shrubs. The

## ESSENTIALS

- Good intermingling with other perennials and around the base of shrubs. Many geraniums smother weeds well; some are superb in containers or tumbling over low walls.

- Most are happy in partial shade and any reasonable soil, but check the needs of each to be sure.

- Cut back at the end of the season (or after winter for evergreen types). Divide and replant if vigor starts to fail.

◀ ◁ 'Blue Sunrise' ('Blogold') makes a billowing plant, ideal in a large container. It is a star from the day the first red-edged yellow shoots peep through, and its bright yellow foliage retains its color as the blue flowers open.

◁ ◀ The dark, prettily veined foliage of 'Dusky Rose' trails over walls, never becoming a nuisance, and keeps its color well right through the season.

# ornamental grasses

perennial

- *spring to winter foliage*
- *summer and fall flowers*

*Elegant combinations of fine qualities, spread across the seasons*

Ornamental grasses (and their relations the sedges) continue to grow in popularity and with good reason: they're so versatile, adapted to many styles of gardens and many situations, and so unexpectedly varied in their qualities. They fall into two groups. Warm season grasses start into growth and flower relatively late; in some climates their flowers may fail to show themselves off before winter. These include hakone grass (*Hakonechloa*), halfa grass (*Imperata*), maiden grass (*Miscanthus*), switch grass (*Panicum*), and fountain grass (*Pennisetum*). Cool season grasses start into growth relatively early, often with attractive new shoots, then flower in summer. They tend to rest in the heat of summer unless watered, and by late summer many are starting to look autumnal. These include feather reed grass (*Calamagrostis*), tufted hair grass (*Deschampsia*), woodrush (*Luzula*), and moor grass (*Molinia*).

Many, both warm season and cool season, feature the familiar slender green foliage that associates so well with neighboring plants with broad leaves and those with a lacy look. Then in fall, the grasses take on their autumn coloring of yellow, tan, beige, and biscuit tones. Using plants from both groups will ensure a long succession of interest.

*Calamagrostis ×acutiflora* has slender, dark green leaves that turn bright yellow in fall, and its upright purple-tinted flowerheads age to tan. 'Overdam' has narrow cream stripes and pinkish flowers; 'Karl Foerster' is taller, with pinkish flowers.

*Deschampsia cespitosa* is evergreen (in warmer areas), with slightly bluish green leaves, hosting a haze of silvered purple flowers, turning bronze or gold later. 'Bronze Veil' ('Bronzeschleier') has flowers that mature to deep bronze; 'Northern Lights' has cream-striped leaves with pink

▶ Many ornamental grasses and sedges develop a new late look as their summer growth matures into a warm autumnal display. *Pennisetum alopecuroides* and *Miscanthus sinensis* feature here.

or purplish leaves, turning yellow in fall and then silvery tan, and pink flowers on upright stems; 'Shenandoah' has good blue leaves and impressive vinous purple fall color.

Pennisetums are renowned for their good fall color and fountain habit: arching flower stems over clumps of similarly arching leaves. *Pennisetum alopecuroides* 'Hameln' is short, with creamy white flowers and fine fall color; *P. orientale* 'Karley Rose' has astonishing deep pink flowers over dark foliage, which turns yellow in fall.

*Calamagrostis ×acutiflora* **'Karl Foerster'**
 Z5–9
 6 × 2ft
 1.8 × 0.6m

*Calamagrostis ×acutiflora* **'Overdam'**
 Z5–9
 4 × 2ft
 1.2 × 0.6m

*Deschampsia cespitosa* **'Bronze Veil' ('Bronzeschleier')**
 Z5–9
 4 × 2ft
 1.2 × 0.6m

*Deschampsia cespitosa* **'Northern Lights'**
 Z5–9
 14 × 10in
 35 × 25cm

*Hakonechloa macra* **'Aureola'**
 Z5–9
 14 × 16in
 35 × 40cm

*Hakonechloa macra* **'Nicolas'**
 Z5–9
 14 × 16in
 35 × 40cm

*Imperata cylindrica* **'Rubra' ('Red Baron')**
 Z6–9
 16 × 12in
 40 × 30cm

*Luzula sylvatica* **'Hohe Tatra'**
 Z5–9
 18 × 18in
 45 × 45cm

*Miscanthus sinensis* **'Adagio'**
 Z5–8
 4 × 2ft
 1.2 × 0.6m

*Miscanthus sinensis* 'Cabaret'
  Z5–8
  6 × 3ft
  1.8 × 0.9m

*Miscanthus sinensis* 'Strictus'
  Z5–8
  6 × 2ft
  1.8 × 0.6m

*Miscanthus sinensis*
  'Variegatus'
  Z5–8
  7 × 3ft
  2.1 × 0.9m

*Molinia caerulea* 'Transparent'
  Z5–9
  6 × 2ft
  1.8 × 0.6m

*Molinia caerulea* 'Variegata'
  Z5–9
  18 × 16in
  45 × 40cm

*Panicum virgatum* 'Heavy
Metal'
  Z5–9
  3 × 3ft
  90 × 90cm

*Panicum virgatum*
  'Shenandoah'
  Z5–9
  4 × 4ft
  1.2 × 1.2m

*Pennisetum alopecuroides*
  'Hameln'
  Z5–9
  2 × 2ft
  60 × 60cm

*Pennisetum orientale* 'Karley
Rose'
  Z6–10
  3 × 3ft
  90 × 90cm

◀ ◁ *Imperata cylindrica* 'Rubra' (Japanese blood grass) moves from red-tipped through completely red to coppery in winter.

◁ ◀ In late summer, the striped leaves of *Miscanthus sinensis* 'Variegatus' are topped with reddish plumes then, in fall and through the winter, the whole plant takes on a new look.

## *Hamamelis*

# witch hazel

**deciduous shrub**

- *fragrant winter and spring flowers*
- *fall foliage color*

*Chosen well, witch hazels are amongst the best of all multi-season shrubs*

Emblematic of the season's turn, the large and colorful spidery flowers of Asian witch hazels, *H. mollis* and its hybrid *H. ×intermedia*, brighten bare branches in late winter and early spring. Each flower has four slender, slightly twisted petals up to twenty times as long as wide; with up to five flowers in each close cluster, and clusters at every

► ▷ The fragrant winter flowers of 'Pallida' are never damaged by snow. They give way to bold foliage, which turns bright and buttery in the autumn.

▷ ► The large red and yellow flowers of 'Aurora' are followed by this intense fall color.

## ESSENTIALS

• Grasses and sedges are good companions: the slender leaves of silvery blue grasses falling across silvered or purplish heucheras is lovely. Ferns, especially the silvery athyriums, make delightful partners.

• Good drainage is crucial. Heucheras vary in their need for sun or shade, but the sunnier their site, the more consistent must be their supply of moisture.

• Weevils are the main pests; the C-shaped white grubs munch through the crown so that, one day, the top growth just blows away. Effective biological control is now available, and chickens love the grubs. Buy from a specialist who will have taken precautions against this nasty little pest. Replant deeper after winter frost heaves.

◀ The transformation in 'Caramel' from the toffee tones of summer to the astonishing purple-backed green foliage of winter is invaluable, especially in a small space.

▲ The silvered purple foliage of 'Jade Gloss' is an all-year feature, enlivened for many weeks by short but well-filled spikes of pale pink flowers.

# foamy bells

**perennial**

- *evergreen foliage*
- *spring flowers*

*Valued especially for the foliage, changing season by season, and the spring flowers*

▶ In spring and summer, the jagged, prettily silvered foliage of 'Kimono' is marked with a chocolatey central stripe.

Although these hybrids between *Heuchera* and *Tiarella* bring together features from both, they also have their own distinctive character. As with heucheras, one of the most valuable features of heucherellas is the tendency of the best to change their foliage color through the year; the precise coloring is partly governed by the plant's inherent qualities and partly by weather conditions: a cool spell in summer may bring on autumnal hues. In addition, many also feature delightful spring flowers; these are sterile and never set seed, so tend to keep blooming for longer than those of either of the parents.

'Alabama Sunrise' features yellow spring foliage with vivid red veining seeping out into the leaf. As summer ripens into autumn, the leaves become greener, while retaining the red veins, then turn pinkish in winter. Unusually tolerant of heat and humidity.

'Brass Lantern' is a large, bold plant with white flowers in spring; it is unusually glossy in that season, when the leaves tend to red along the veins and gold at the edge. In summer and into autumn the foliage becomes richer and duller in tone, then in winter develops tan and almost chocolate tones.

'Kimono' is a worldwide favorite. In spring, the new leaves are chartreuse with brownish crimson veins, then in summer the color matures to silvery green with a crimson central vein and a network of dark green side veins. It turns rosier in winter. Spikes of white spring flowers are a welcome extra.

'Quicksilver' not only features changing foliage but good white flowers, opening from pink buds and carried on dark stems. Dark bronze spring foliage matures to silvery green in summer. Unusually tough and vigorous.

'Sweet Tea' is a bold plant with large, apricot leaves in spring, each with a blood red center. Richer and darker foliage coloring develops in summer, and russet and cinnamon tones dominate until fall, when cool weather again brings brighter shades.

## ESSENTIALS

- Lovely as container specimens in rich compost, and in shade gardens.

- Partial or dappled shade is ideal, with a humus-rich soil that does not dry out. Heucherellas vary enormously in their vigor and resilience in tough, especially dry, conditions.

- Cut back old foliage at the end of winter to allow sight of fresh new leaves. Mulch annually in spring.

×*Heucherella* 'Alabama Sunrise'
Z4–9
20 × 12in
50 × 30cm

×*Heucherella* 'Brass Lantern'
Z4–9
10 × 16in
25 × 40cm

×*Heucherella* 'Kimono'
Z4–9
10 × 16in
25 × 40cm

×*Heucherella* 'Quicksilver'
Z4–9
14 × 16in
35 × 40cm

×*Heucherella* 'Sweet Tea'
Z4–9
28 × 20in
70 × 50cm

◀ In winter, everything changes for 'Kimono' as the leaves take on a more dramatic look.

▲ The unusual summer copper and brass coloring of 'Brass Lantern' turns richer in fall.

# funkia

**perennial**

We all know hostas. No shade garden is complete without one, or many more than one. They have four features of value to gardeners. Firstly, large hostas in general and the forms related to *H. sieboldiana* in particular are often very impressive as their new shoots emerge from the soil in spring—fat and exciting spikes, with hints of color to come. This is the stage when slugs can be devastating—one tiny bite at this stage becomes a gaping hole as the leaf matures and expands.

The leaf unrolls, and shows off its first color. In some hostas, the first color sets the tone for the season; in others, the coloring changes during the summer. Many hostas flower, though some are far from impressive in that respect, but the best not only hold their flowers above the foliage so they are shown off effectively but are also scented.

Then, in fall, comes the feature that so many gardeners forget: fall foliage color. Some hostas, including 'Christmas Tree' and other Sieboldiana types, are transformed in autumn into exciting buttery shades or rich biscuit and tawny coloring, colors that fit well into the fall palette of tree and shrub coloring. Hosta fall color is at its best and lasts the longest in cool conditions—but without a frost; so in some seasons it may last for many weeks, in some it can be cut short to just a few days, or, sadly, not happen at all.

A few examples will give you a taste of the combinations of features on show from just one variety.

'Blue Mouse Ears' is a neat charmer with, from spring to fall, heavy-textured, relatively slug-resistant, blue leaves turned up at the edges. In summer short spikes of large lavender blue flowers create a harmonious pairing.

'Christmas Tree' has broad, dark green leaves with a yellow margin in spring which fades to cream in summer. Lavender midsummer flowers are followed by fat reddish purple seedpods; in fall the foliage turns butter yellow with a creamy edge.

'Devon Green' features lustrous deep green corrugated

- *spring shoots*
- *spring to fall foliage*
- *fragrant summer flowers*
- *fall foliage color*

*Essential shade perennials with real three-season presence*

foliage with a pale midrib, especially at the base, and smoky lilac flowers like those of 'Halcyon'. Then in fall the whole plant turns gold with rusty overtones.

'Fragrant Bouquet' has slightly wavy, pale green leaves with yellow edges that fade to creamy white; and in late summer and early autumn, 3in/7.5cm, palest lavender, almost white flowers are held well above the leaves on vertical stems. The flowers are amongst the most fragrant of all hostas.

'Great Expectations' has attractive emerging shoots, bold yellow-splashed foliage, very slug-resistant leaves, and summer flowers. Makes an impressive, if slow growing specimen.

## ESSENTIALS

- Early in the season, nearby plants should not hide the beauty of the emerging shoots; a fresh application of mulch may make the best background. The feathery foliage of ferns and the slender leaves of irises and daffodils make good partners.

- Rich, moist but not waterlogged soil in dappled or partial shade is ideal. The more consistently moist the soil, the more sun hostas will take. Many are also lovely in containers.

- Protect from slugs. Water in dry weather. Do not split the clumps regularly, as is often recommended for perennials; leave them to develop into mature specimens.

◀ ◁ The neat little cupped leaves of 'Blue Mouse Ears' host short summer spikes of flowers.

◁ ◀ Many hostas simply fade away in fall, but the transformation in 'Christmas Tree' is really exciting and brings new light and color to the autumn garden.

# hydrangea

**deciduous shrub**

- *spring to fall foliage*
- *summer and fall flowers*

*A diversity of tough easy-to-grow types, with flowers and foliage in evolving colors*

Everyone knows hydrangeas, but not all gardeners are aware of the fascinating possibilities amongst what is an unexpectedly varied range. Representatives of *H. macrophylla* (big-leaf, hortensia, mophead, and lacecap hydrangeas) are available in the greatest number. We are all familiar with the way their flowerheads evolve from pink or blue in their prime into autumnal russet shades, but a few lacecaps add colorful foliage to the mix. 'Maculata' (with white flowers) features leaves irregularly marked in green, gray-green, and white, with the white tending towards the edge of the leaf; 'Quadricolor' adds bright yellow to the mix (and pinkish to lilac flowers); the weaker 'Tricolor' (with pink to pale blue flowers) has foliage marked in two shades, green and cream. But other kinds of hydrangeas are increasingly popular and prove to be fine plants in different ways.

The combination of spectacular summer flowers and the dried winter heads into which they mature is a feature of relatively few shrubs; but along with *H. macrophylla*, *H. arborescens* stands out in this respect, in particular in its selection 'Annabelle', with its huge heads crowded with white flowers. In fact, the flowers are so huge that the stems arch under the load, especially after rain. They mature to green and then remain tawny or bleached white through winter.

*Hydrangea paniculata* (Pee-Gee hydrangea) has impressive cone-shaped flowerheads which, in general, open white or greenish white, then age through blush and rosy shades to deep pink. Most impressive are 'Pink Diamond' ('Interhydia'), 'Pink Lady', and 'Pinky Winky' ('Dvppinky'); yellow fall color, if it occurs, is unremarkable. Pruning of *H. paniculata* varieties has a significant impact on flower size and flowering season.

▶ The flowerheads of 'Pink Lady' start off white, develop pink tinges, and mature to deep pink. Flowering is most dramatic when plants are pruned hard each spring.

# busy Lizzie

annual

- *spring to fall foliage*
- *summer and fall flowers*

*Prettily patterned foliage enhanced by attractive late-season flowers*

▶ The neatly cream-edged foliage and peachy flowers of 'Fusion Peach Frost' ('Balfuspeafro') bring effortless color harmony to any summer container planting.

Of the eight hundred and fifty species of *Impatiens* scattered around most of the world, relatively few combine features that would appeal to the savvy gardener. But amongst those grown as summer annuals, there are some real gems. Most often grown in containers, all combine a long season of attractively marked foliage with flowers in either contrasting or harmonious shades. They come in a variety of styles that are, in essence, classier forms of the seed-raised impatiens so popular for their incessant flowering. And while for many months, both variegated foliage and summer flowers come together in harmony to create attractive combinations, the foliage carries the plant before flowering and when flowering eases off. Three cultivars stand out.

'Fiesta Olé Peppermint' ('Balolespri'), a selection of *I. walleriana*, combines purplish double flowers splashed in white with white-edged foliage. There is indeed a fiesta of attractive foliage combined with unusually long-lasting rosebud flowers. 'Fusion Peach Frost' ('Balfuspeafro') is a fine summer container plant, developed from crossing the familiar garden impatiens with *I. auricoma* and its seashell-shaped flowers. The pouched peachy apricot blooms, maturing almost to pink, are held against pale green foliage prettily edged in cream, a uniquely stylish pairing. Plants make rounded mounds of harmonious color, the flower and leaf variegation uniting to create a restful, satisfying look.

'Masquerade', another *I. walleriana* selection, is for the gardener who never removes the Ray-Bans. Brilliant flowers set against yellow-variegated leaves . . . if you want to be stunned, just watch it grow. This is basically a spreading, dramatically variegated form of an everyday red impatiens. If the brilliance of the combination offends you, there are others who will love it. There are heirlooms in a similar style, although all make large, shy-flowering plants compared with modern sorts.

- Around irises with purplish spring growth, try low-growing bright and gold variegated *Ajuga reptans* 'Toffee Chip' or the creeping, yellow-leaved *Lysimachia nummularia* 'Aurea'. Pair variegated types with another powerhouse perennial, *Amsonia hubrichtii*.

- Most prefer full sun and moist soil, although they often perform well, if less vigorously, in soil that, although not wet, is rarely dry. *Iris pallida* is happy in drier conditions.

- All benefit from dead-heading and may need dividing and replanting after a few years. Most will need old foliage removed in fall.

◀ Before and after these rich purple-blue flowers, the striped foliage of *I. laevigata* 'Variegata' makes a bright impact.

▲ The yellow-striped foliage of *I. pallida* 'Variegata', dramatic in its own right, is enhanced by a brief burst of blue, early summer flowers.

## ESSENTIALS

- Fades away early, so plants such as autumn asters that will spread to occupy its space are ideally planted nearby.

- Best in moist but not waterlogged soil and in partial shade. New growth is frost tender: avoid frost pockets and provide shelter from early icy winds.

- Tidy away old foliage as it deteriorates and ensure that winter debris is cleared from the crown in late winter, so the new shoots are revealed.

◀ The red stems and golden yellow foliage of 'Gold Heart' light up the spring garden with their vibrant coloring from when the shoots first emerge.

▲ The pink lockets of *L. spectabilis* hang daintily along the length of the arching stems.

# honeysuckle

**deciduous vine**

- *fragrant spring flowers*
- *summer and fall foliage*
- *fall fruits*

*Those flowers are famous for their scent, but there are berries and foliage, too*

Honeysuckle vines have several valuable ornamental features. The best of the flared tubular flowers produce that exquisite heavy fragrance that not only entrances us as we relax outside in the evening but also attracts moths, with which they are popular as a food source. A few feature variegated foliage, and most also develop clusters of berries in summer or fall. The fruiting of honeysuckles can be unpredictable both in its occurrence and in the time for which the berries remain on the plant; they may disappear in a week or two or last for months. It seems their appeal to birds may depend on the available alternatives.

'Graham Thomas' is very vigorous with cream flowers turning white over a long period, red berries, and exceptional fragrance.

'Harlequin' ('Sherlite') has reddish flower buds opening to white flowers maturing to yellow and with leaves edged in cream. Less scented than many.

'Scentsation' has clusters of well-scented white flowers, fading to rich cream, followed by rich red berries.

'Sweet Sue' is modest in growth, with prolific white flowers turning cream, red berries, and a wonderful fragrance.

Unfortunately, variegated foliage is mainly found on *L. japonica*, reviled in North America for its invasive tendencies. In Britain it has established itself only recently, mainly in the south, but has not yet proved to be a problem. 'Aureoreticulata' has unusually small, white fragrant flowers maturing to yellow, with black berries, and the veins on each leaf are picked out in gold. 'Maskerade' has creamy margins to the leaves and fragrant rosy flowers, which are white within, turning into black berries. 'Mint Crisp' has foliage brightly mottled in pale yellow, becoming pinkish in fall; white fragrant flowers become yellow as they age.

▶ The fragrant flowers of 'Graham Thomas' are open over a long period and followed by clusters of scarlet red berries.

## ESSENTIALS

- Plant on arches or trellises, by doorways, on poles in borders—anywhere the fragrance can be appreciated. Low branches of mature trees can be hosts for vigorous varieties.

- Happy in rich but well-drained soil, *L. japonica* is more adaptable and takes more sun than forms of *L. periclymenum*, which dislikes drought and appreciates a little shade.

- If necessary, prune in autumn when the berries are gone, shortening the strongest shoots by two-thirds. Watch for aphids.

*Lonicera ×italica* 'Harlequin' ('Sherlite')
Z4–9
10–12 × 3–6ft
3–3.5 × 0.9–1.8m

*Lonicera japonica* 'Aureoreticulata'
Z4–10
20 × 8ft
6 × 2.4m

*Lonicera japonica* 'Maskerade'
Z4–10
20 × 8ft
6 × 2.4m

*Lonicera japonica* 'Mint Crisp'
Z4–10
20 × 8ft
6 × 2.4m

*Lonicera periclymenum* 'Graham Thomas'
Z5–9
20 × 8ft
6 × 2.4m

*Lonicera periclymenum* 'Scentsation'
Z5–9
30 × 10ft
9 × 3m

*Lonicera periclymenum* 'Sweet Sue'
Z5–9
10 × 6ft
3 × 1.8m

◀ Clusters of shining red berries follow the exceptionally fragrant flowers of 'Scentsation'.

# crabapple                    *Malus*

**deciduous tree**

Crabapple trees are survivors. Old trees flower and fruit prolifically in hedges, in derelict gardens, and by roadsides, even when plagued with disease. So varieties from long ago are still to be found—although identifying them is difficult—and because the seeds are spread by birds, the trees we come across along roadsides and elsewhere often are unnamed seedlings.

Their fluttering spring flowers, many fragrant, and prolific fall fruits are the crabapple's main features, but new growth can be appealingly bronzed or purple-tinted. Summer foliage too may bring valuable sultry tones, and in some varieties the fall color is gorgeous. And those autumn "apples" are not only attractive but edible: birds will eat every kind, and a lot of them are delicious to us as well.

In flower, crabapples vary from pure white through a vast array of pink shades to reddish purple. Buds may be almost scarlet, but the open flowers are never quite in that shade. Different varieties flower at different times, from early to mid spring into early summer. Whatever the season, flowering comes in a dramatic burst and may be as short as a few days or as long as two weeks, depending on the climate and weather. Double-flowered varieties are sometimes seen but are less popular; they flower for a day or two longer, but I'm not sure that such a minimally extended flowering season is worth the lack of elegance in the blooms. One useful thing to remember about them all: if flowering overlaps, they will pollinate nearby cooking and eating apple trees.

And then there's the fruits: from ¼in/6mm to 2in/5cm across and varying dramatically in color from limey green, through every shade of yellow and gold, often tinted with pink or red shades, then into orange and red tones, burgundy, and purple. Varieties with large numbers of small fruits can be as colorful as those with fewer, larger ones.

Many, especially older varieties, make large trees; while in flower, the spectacle and the fragrance may be impressive, but not all gardens can take such an imposing specimen—especially as crabapples tend

- *spring shoots*
- *spring or summer flowers*
- *summer and fall foliage*
- *edible fall fruits*

*Tough, reliable garden trees, with an unbeatable array of attractive features*

193

to cast deep shade over a long season. More recently, much smaller varieties have been introduced, some sufficiently compact to grow as standards in containers on the patio or deck. So, how to choose? This is my selection of species and hybrids, in a range of sizes and balancing the best flowers, foliage, and fruits.

Of the species, *M. floribunda* offers a striking combination of carmine red, almost scarlet, buds and white spring flowers followed by ¾in/2cm red-blushed yellow fruits, much enjoyed by birds; in *M.*

◄ *Malus floribunda* presents a spectacular combination of brilliant red buds opening to white flowers.

▲ The long-lasting fruits of 'Red Sentinel' brighten a relatively upright tree.

## ESSENTIALS

- Crabapples can make splendid specimen trees and are good along boundaries and in corners, but beware their dense shade. A mature tree is an ideal host for a rambling rose.

- Happy in sun or a little shade, and in any soil that is not waterlogged.

- Support is important for newly planted trees. Disease can be a problem; although never fatal, it can slow the development of newly planted specimens, so be prepared with a fungicide.

- Crabapple varieties are grafted onto roots that can control the eventual size of the tree. An increasing range of rootstocks is available, so it always pays to check labels and take the advice of a good nursery to be sure your tree will mature to the size you need. 'Evereste', for example, on a dwarfing rootstock, will mature at only about 4ft/1.2m in a large container. Dimensions for it and others, on normal rootstock in the open ground, follow.

*hupehensis*, pink buds open to fragrant, white early summer flowers followed by ½in/1cm cherry red fruits.

'Evereste' ('Perpetu'). Red buds open to clouds of white flowers followed by 1in/2.5cm red-speckled orange fruits.

'Golden Hornet'. White spring flowers are followed by bright yellow, slightly conical 1in/2.5cm fruits that last until the turn of the year.

'John Downie'. Pink buds open to white flowers, followed by large (1¼in/3cm) oranged-red fruits. Considered the best for jelly.

'Prairie Fire'. Maroon early growth matures to deep green; the red buds open to pinkish red flowers; tiny (⅜in/9mm) reddish purple fruits follow.

'Profusion'. Coppery red new shoots, large (½in/1cm) fragrant burgundy flowers, deep red fruits.

'Red Sentinel'. White, late spring flowers and heavy crops of very long-lasting bright red 1in/2.5cm fruits until late winter.

▶ 'Profusion' features cop-
▷ pery red new spring shoots
and persistent red fruits, as well
as these richly colored flowers.

▷ The yellow fruits of 'Golden
▶ Hornet', following white
spring flowers, can be so prolific as to weigh down the
autumn branches.

*Malus* 'Evereste' ('Perpetu')
Z5–8
4–10 × 3–8ft
1.2–3 × 0.9–2.4m

*Malus floribunda*
Z4–8
30 × 30ft
9 × 9m

*Malus hupehensis*
Z5–8
40 × 40ft
12 × 12m

*Malus* 'John Downie'
Z5–8
30 × 20ft
9 × 6m

*Malus* ×*moerlandsii* 'Profusion'
Z4–8
30 × 30ft
9 × 9m

*Malus* 'Prairie Fire'
Z5–8
20 × 20ft
6 × 6m

*Malus* ×*robusta* 'Red Sentinel'
Z4–8
13–26 × 13–26ft
4–8 × 4–8m

*Malus* ×*zumi* 'Golden Hornet'
Z5–8
28 × 25ft
8.5 × 8m

▲ *Malus hupehensis* is another of those crabapples that packs a "small but many" fruit punch.

## Meconopsis    # Himalayan poppy

**perennial**

• *winter rosette*

• *summer flowers*

*Gorgeous winter rosettes in unique colorings give way to towers of flowers*

▶ The extraordinary golden hairy rosettes of 'Ginger Nut', a form of *M. paniculata*, a yellow-flowered species.

The Himalayan poppies bring us some of the most gorgeous of perennials—both for foliage and for flowers. At their best they provide both overwintering rosettes of hairy leaves in colors seen in no other plants and impressive heads of four-petalled poppy flowers in blues, yellows, or reds.

Two stand out for being the easiest to grow and having the most impressive rosettes and most colorful flowers: *M. napaulensis* and *M. paniculata*. It is only fair to say, however, that these are not tough and easy perennials in the style of, say, hostas or echinaceas. Firstly, both these species have an unusual growth pattern: plants develop over a number of years, increasing in size with their evergreen rosettes of foliage becoming ever more impressive. Then they flower. Then they die. Both species are rather variable, so check nursery tags and catalog descriptions carefully before buying. They will also hybridize with each other, and often plants sold under either name are hybrids. If the leaves look good, buy the plant.

*Meconopsis napaulensis* features rosettes up to 2ft/60cm across for up to four or even six years, each leaf covered in silvery or yellowish hairs and lobed in varying degrees. The large rosettes formed in the year before the plants flower are simply amazing; the towers of pink or red flowers which then develop occasionally reach 8ft/2.4m.

*Meconopsis paniculata* is similar though shorter in flower, with rosettes of foliage covered in silvery, golden, or gingery hairs and each leaf up to 2ft/60cm long, making a huge rosette. Running up to flower rather more quickly, after two or three years, the flowers are usually bright canary yellow.

The fabled blue-flowered Himalayan poppies are generally less fussy but are not evergreen and are without the gorgeous silver or gingery coloring. Although the foliage of *M. betonicifolia* may be covered in rusty hairs, plants are short-lived. 'Lingholm' has attractive, narrow leaves without hairs. Both have blue flowers.

## ESSENTIALS

- Good as a small garden specimen and as foundation planting. Smaller varieties can be planted together as ground cover or even in classy planters.

- Develops the best leaf color in full sun but will also grow in shade. Happy in any soil, including dry conditions once established, but prefers fertile soil.

- Little care is needed; the oldest growth can be cut out at the base each year if not cut for the house.

◀ The early growth on the dwarf 'Fire Power', a scrumptious strawberry ice cream shade, is followed by white flowers and red berries.

▶ On most varieties, crowded clusters of red berries follow the white flowers and weigh down the branches.

*Nandina domestica*
Z6–9
6 × 5ft
1.8 × 1.5m

*Nandina domestica* 'Fire Power'
Z6–9
18 × 24in
45 × 60cm

*Nandina domestica* 'Harbor Dwarf'
Z6–9
3 × 4ft
0.9 × 1.2m

*Nandina domestica* 'Plum Passion' ('Monum')
Z6–9
4–5 × 2–3ft
1.2–1.5 × 0.6–0.9m

*Nandina domestica* 'Richmond'
Z6–9
6 × 5ft
1.8 × 1.5m

## Paeonia

# peony

**perennial or deciduous shrub**

- *spring shoots*
- *summer flowers*
- *fall foliage color and fruits*

*Not just those flowers but many phases, in a few short months, from shoots to fruits*

▶ 'Sarah Bernhardt', a classic peony, opens with colorful spring growth followed by large and fragrant flowers.

Peonies produce some of the most sumptuous and dramatic of all flowers, and many gardeners are content to grow them for just that relatively fleeting display. But peonies can bring more, far more, features to sunny situations. As they first peep through the soil, the shoots of many herbaceous peonies glisten with deep red. Next come the globular buds, visible in the tips of the shoots, some of which may still hold their early coloring; and many tree peonies have very striking buds on individual stems. Leaves too are an attractive feature, from repeatedly dissected to broad and bold, a few with a bluish cast on the upper surface. Of course, the blooms are magical—single or double or in a range of other forms, sometimes in one pure shade, sometimes boldly marked, and often attractively scented. As summer fades to fall, many plants feature unmistakable fat seedpods, a few splitting to reveal colorful seeds and interiors, and some even develop attractive autumnal foliage tones. And, increasingly,

peonies are appreciated as fresh or dried cut flowers.

*Paeonia cambessedesii* has extraordinary, heavily veined, reddish purple shoots emerging in spring and opening to broad, silvery blue foliage, which is red on the back. The pink or magenta single flowers open in late spring and are followed by seedpods, which split to reveal the highly distinctive combination of blue-black seeds set against a reddish background. Perfect for dry and sunny places, but slow.

*Paeonia lactiflora* is the species to which most of the familiar garden peonies belong, and many feature red emerging shoots and young growth that fades to green by the time the fragrant flowers open. Especially excellent are 'Sarah Bernhardt' and 'Whitleyi Major', with its red fall foliage, but there are many others.

*Paeonia mlokosewitchii* has new shoots in reddish coral becoming coppery or smoky purple and green with smoky tints when the lovely, single yellow flowers open. Later, the seedpods split to reveal blue-black seeds against a vivid

## ESSENTIALS

- Ensure these perennial border favorites are not overshadowed by tall neighbors. Some are good in drought and gravel gardens.

- Most peonies enjoy full sun and a well-drained but rich and fertile soil, but many will also thrive in bright light without full sun. Plant in the fall, and prepare the soil well.

- Cut back the old growth in late fall (except tree peonies), mulch before new shoots emerge. Best left to mature into impressive clumps.

▶ Finely dissected foliage makes *P. tenuifolia* a lovely foliage plant even before its red buds and flowers appear. When the flowers fade, the inflated seedpods are the next attraction.

red background, and coppery orange fall foliage follows.

*Paeonia obovata* features new shoots in pinkish red, slightly coppery at times, and the leaves often still have a purplish or darkly coppery tone when the white or pink single flowers open. The seedpods split to reveal blue seeds against a red background. The stars are var. *alba* (with pure white flowers) and var. *willmottiae* (with red stems, bluish leaves that are red underneath, and white flowers).

*Paeonia suffruticosa* is the tree peony, of which there are many with purplish young growth, huge single or double flowers, and then reddish foliage in autumn.

*Paeonia tenuifolia* is distinctive in its repeatedly divided foliage, and the new shoots look like purple old-fashioned shaving brushes. As the leaves become dark green, deep red single flowers open. Even after the petals drop, the plant is still impressive for its foliage and seedpods.

*Paeonia*

▲ As the foliage turns to green, the large and vivid flowers of tree peonies (here, 'Wu Long Peng Sheng') open to provide a very different display.

◄ Tree peonies offer several charms, beginning with their early purplish foliage, as here on 'Wu Long Peng Sheng'.

up then ensures that flowers are produced more prolifically than on spring-sown plants. In some, the winter leaves are finely cut, almost lacy, in grayish or silvery tones as well as green; in others the foliage is broader and may be steely gray blue in color. After the flowers come the seedpods, which are themselves extremely attractive in some varieties, and then the seed is shed and germinates to provide plants for the following year.

*Papaver rhoeas* is the European corn poppy, with rosettes of bristly, prettily divided

## ESSENTIALS

• Allow poppies to self-sow in mixed borders, wildflower gardens, or gravel gardens.

• Best in full sun and any reasonable soil that is not wet in winter. *Papaver rhoeas* and *P. somniferum* may need support in rich conditions.

• Thin seedlings to 12in/30cm, remove off-types amongst self-sown plants, and if they self-sow too prolifically, deadhead before the seed is shed.

◀ ◁ From a summer or autumn sowing, the bold foliage of *P. somniferum* is impressive.

◁ ◀ 'Burgundy Frills' provides a succession of these captivating flowers.

leaves and single or sometimes double summer flowers. 'Mother of Pearl', in pastel shades with no bright reds, is the pick, and look out for the double-flowered 'Angel's Choir' in similar soft shades.

*Papaver somniferum* is the opium poppy, grown in gardens in a wide range of forms for both its foliage and flowers. All feature broad, rather heavily textured, lobed leaves in bluish or grayish tones, making a dramatic rosette that is followed by very large single or double flowers, up to 6in/15cm across, sometimes blotched or fringed, as in 'Burgundy Frills'. There is even a form selected for its especially large seedpods, which can be dried for the winter. It's important to note that, according to the U.S. Controlled Substances Act, knowingly growing *P. somniferum* is punishable by a fine of up to $1 million and a prison term of up to twenty years. Perhaps that's why some, but not all, seed companies list it as *P. paeoniflorum*.

*Papaver triniifolium* is a true biennial: sow in spring or summer to flower the following year. Less often seen, it is by far the best for its repeatedly dissected bluish leaf rosettes, followed by soft orange flowers over a long period.

**Papaver rhoeas**
Z3–8
30 × 12in
75 × 30cm

**Papaver rhoeas 'Angel's Choir'**
Z3–8
30 × 12in
75 × 30cm

**Papaver rhoeas 'Mother of Pearl'**
Z3–8
30 × 12in
75 × 30cm

**Papaver somniferum 'Burgundy Frills'**
Z4–9
5 × 1ft
1.5 × 0.3m

**Papaver triniifolium**
Z6–8
15 × 12in
38 × 30cm

# border phlox

## *Phlox*

**perennial**

Most border phlox (*P. paniculata*) have a sumptuous summer season of flowers and fragrance, which ensures their place in both formal and informal borders. But add variegated foliage, and you have a whole new dimension—of contrast or of harmony. The brightness of the variegated foliage (in all cases, the leaves have a pale cream or yellow edge, not center) catches the eye from the first week of

- *spring shoots*
- *spring to fall foliage*
- *fragrant summer flowers*

*Striking variegated foliage with a summer burst of outstandingly fragrant flowers*

◀ 'Blue Evening' has intriguingly colorful new spring shoots, followed by strongly fragrant flowers held on appealingly dark stems.

tints, sometimes emerging almost black. As the shoots start to extend and the leaves unroll, they become greener; but often, even as the flowers start to open, the stems remain purple or almost black, bringing a whole new style to the plant. The popular 'Blue Paradise' and the very similar 'Blue Evening', with its extraordinary fragrance, are the pick of these. The new shoots are best shown off against a pale gravel mulch—a dark organic mulch does not provide enough contrast. In flower, both are a good mid blue in color, with some white flecks, and not too tall or floppy.

 'Norah Leigh' brings us months of softly variegated foliage before the flowers open.

▷ ▶ The colorful new shoots of 'Becky Towe' carry carmine flowers later in the season.

*Phlox paniculata* 'Becky Towe'
Z4–8
3–4 × 2–3ft
0.9–1.2 × 0.6–0.9m

*Phlox paniculata* 'Blue Evening'
Z4–8
3–4 × 2–3ft
0.9–1.2 × 0.6–0.9m

*Phlox paniculata* 'Blue Paradise'
Z4–8
3–4 × 2–3ft
0.9–1.2 × 0.6–0.9m

*Phlox paniculata* 'Goldmine'
Z4–8
3–4 × 2–3ft
0.9–1.2 × 0.6–0.9m

*Phlox paniculata* 'Harlequin'
Z4–8
3–4 × 2–3ft
0.9–1.2 × 0.6–0.9m

*Phlox paniculata* 'Norah Leigh'
Z4–8
3–4 × 2–3ft
0.9–1.2 × 0.6–0.9m

# Japanese andromeda

**evergreen shrub**

- *evergreen foliage*
- *spring shoots and flowers*

*Essential flowering evergreens, spring-loaded with extra powerhouse features*

Apart from being one of the most dependably deer-resistant shrubs we have, Japanese andromeda is an attractive spring-flowering evergreen with colorful new growth in the same season. The new shoots are often in tawny brown or pale olive shades, but in the best varieties, they are a brilliant red, almost scarlet. The spring coloring may coincide with the white (usually) bells of flowers, or it may come

▶ ▷ When well sited, the variegated 'Carnaval' has impressive strings of white flowers in spring and subtly pink-tinted winter foliage.

▷ ▶ The new shoots of 'Katsura' are followed by scented pink flowers.

## ESSENTIALS

- Taller types make fine back-of-the-border or boundary specimens; more compact types are good in containers and raised beds.

- All require acid soil and are happy in partial or dappled shade or even full sun in moist conditions. Variegated forms may flower poorly, if at all, unless grown in good light and moist, fertile soil.

- No pruning necessary, except occasionally to improve their shape; usually best left to grow naturally.

shortly before or after; and any second, later flushes will show that same bright, new-growth color. Other features of interest include bronzed winter foliage or colorful flower buds that wait through the winter to burst in spring. There are some lovely variegated forms as well.

'Carnaval' is a variegated form of 'Mountain Fire' with bright red new shoots, white flowers, and subtly pink-tinted winter foliage.

'Dorothy Wyckoff' combines bronzed winter leaves with wine red overwintering flower buds, followed by white flowers opening from pink buds and contrasting with their dark red stems.

'Flaming Silver' has bright red unvariegated shoots that mature to pink-edged green and then to a silvery white margin, plus creamy white flowers.

'Forest Flame' is the best known pieris, with bright red young growth turning pink to creamy white to green and large drooping clusters of white flowers.

'Katsura' has slightly bronzed, deep red shoots in spring, followed by unusually long strings of gently scented, pale pink flowers. Tolerant of poor soil and summer heat.

'Little Heath' is a compact form with small leaves whose new pink shoots are lovely set against the creamy-edged leaves.

'Mountain Fire' has vivid red new shoots that mature through chestnut brown and coppery green to green, with bright white flowers.

'Variegata', the most vigorous variegated form, combines new pink shoots, white-edged leaves, and white flowers.

*Pieris* 'Flaming Silver'
Z5–8
3–4 × 3–4ft
0.9–1.2 × 0.9–1.2m

*Pieris* 'Forest Flame'
Z6–9
4–8 × 4–8ft
1.2–2.4 × 1.2–2.4m

*Pieris japonica* 'Carnaval'
Z5–8
7 × 4ft
2.1 × 1.2m

*Pieris japonica* 'Dorothy Wyckoff'
Z5–8
4–5 × 4–5ft
1.2–1.5 × 1.2–1.5m

*Pieris japonica* 'Katsura'
Z5–8
5–10 × 5–6ft
1.5–3 × 1.5–1.8m

*Pieris japonica* 'Little Heath'
Z5–8
2–3 × 2–3ft
0.6–0.9 × 0.6–0.9m

*Pieris japonica* 'Mountain Fire'
   Z5–8
   6–10 × 5–8ft
   1.8–3 × 1.5–2.4m

*Pieris japonica* 'Variegata'
   Z6–8
   5–6 × 3–4ft
   1.5–1.8 × 0.9–1.2m

▲ In early spring the red stems and colorful flower buds of many Japanese andromedas look slightly ethereal coated in clear ice.

## *Podophyllum*

# mayapple

**perennial**

- *spring shoots and flowers*
- *spring and summer foliage*
- *summer fruits*

*This easy, attractive native woodlander squeezes many looks into just a few months*

The mayapple, *Podophyllum peltatum*, is a familiar eastern North American woodlander, native from Quebec in the north to Florida and Texas in the south. Clearly, an adaptable plant! And it packs several features into its short growing season. As the soil first starts to warm, the shoots burst through. The folded embryonic foliage is wrapped around the stem, and continuing growth soon takes the green flower

▶ ▷ The emerging spring shoots of the pink form of *P. peltatum* show the young flower bud topping folded bronzed leaves, which open to a broad green summer canopy.

▷ ▶ Usually the flowers of *P. peltatum* are white, but the pink form opens with a show of bronzed young foliage.

222

## ESSENTIALS

- Splendid ground cover in woodland shade; can become too vigorous, crowding less pugnacious neighbors.

- Happiest in dappled or partial shade in a humus-rich soil.

- Ensure that neighboring plants do not encroach and mask the emerging shoots. Cut the whole plant back as the foliage becomes ragged.

bud to the tip; the whole thing looks like a little hunched-and-cloaked hermit. In the best forms, the new shoots are bright coppery bronze. The plants with bronzed foliage always feature pink flowers—look out for them.

The succulent stems surge upwards, each bearing a pair of rounded leaves that expand and stretch above the fattening flower bud. About 12in/30cm across, each glossy green leaf is split into five to eight lobes, toothed across the outer edge. Below, from the point where the stem splits to carry the two leaves, the single nodding flower opens. Usually white, sometimes cream, and pink-tinted at its prettiest, it seems to hover over a yellow central boss. A form with flowers striped in red has also been recorded and is perhaps more common than is thought: not everyone is inclined to crawl

through the woods, lifting leaves to check mayapple flowers. Alas.

As the weeks pass, the leaves become less fragile and stiffer, and a fat fruit develops from every flower. Plumping to 2in/5cm long and maturing bright yellow by midsummer, the "apples" are edible raw (though said to be better cooked) *when fully ripe*—and not before, else they cause digestive misadventures. (In my experience with our happily extending clump of the bronze-leaved, pink-flowered form, some creature with a cast-iron stomach always eats the fruits before they ripen.) As the fruits ripen, the foliage begins to deteriorate badly, to the point when cutting the whole plant back to the ground for an early dormancy is the most aesthetically pleasing option.

*Podophyllum peltatum*
   Z5–9
   18in × 4ft
   45cm × 1.2m

# Solomon's seal

## *Polygonatum*

**perennial**

Most Solomon's seals exhibit the basic pair of appealing features: they flower and then carry berries. But they do so relatively demurely. One form of these elegant and easy shade perennials, however, outshines all others, making it one of the most treasured of all two-for-one plants. *Polygonatum odoratum* var. *pluriflorum* 'Variegatum' is its name, and although several variegated forms are available (and these

- *spring shoots*
- *spring and summer foliage*
- *summer flowers*
- *fall foliage color and fruits*

*Essential shade lovers, blending subtle and dramatic features from spring to fall*

◀ The subtle variegation of 'Variegatum' harmonizes well with the summer flowers, then in fall the foliage takes on a whole new look.

are good, too), the one with the cumbersome name is the one to look for. So, why?

In spring the new shoots are bright, bold, and instantly capture the attention ("What is that?!"). First a fat, pointed pink shoot emerges. Next, this sheath splits to reveal the first signs of the variegated foliage: two or three rolled gray-green leaves with yellow edges wrapped around each other. The first leaves burst out, and their tips roll outward, showing their bright green and yellow coloring. And then the stems stretch; these too are an important feature, distinguishing this Solomon's seal from other variegated forms: its stems are a striking red early in the season. Glossy green leaves with their cream to white markings arrange themselves alternately along those red stems, by now arching over elegantly, as they extend—quite a picture. Each leaf is delicately edged in creamy white, with a few extra slivers of cream towards the tip.

As the weeks pass, the stem coloring fades, but by then the flowers have opened: green-tipped white bells hang in clusters of two to five, swinging from each leaf joint along the upper half of the stem. Occasionally the flowers drop off as they fade, but sometimes they mature into black berries on slender strings. In fall, the whole plant turns bright yellow.

The other variegated form you may come across is *P. ×hybridum* 'Striatum' ('Grace Barker'), which differs most obviously in the lack of red stems and the leaves being unpredictably streaked and edged in white. It has a long season of brightly marked foliage, green-tipped white bells, and blue fruits—but it doesn't quite have the class of its more ponderously named cousin.

**ESSENTIALS**

- Ideal in the middle ground of the shade garden, especially with ferns.

- Best in moist, humus-rich soil, but *P. odoratum* var. *pluriflorum* 'Variegatum' does surprisingly well in dry shade once established.

- Cut back the old growth before spring and ensure that those dramatic new shoots are not hidden by neighboring plants.

*Polygonatum ×hybridum* 'Striatum' ('Grace Barker')
Z6–9
3–5 × 2–4ft
0.9–1.5 × 0.6–1.2m

*Polygonatum odoratum* var. *pluriflorum* 'Variegatum'
Z3–8
18–24 × 18–30in
45–60 × 45–75cm

◀ 'Striatum' ('Grace Barker') brings us brighter variegation and larger flowers, but no pink shoots or fall color.

▶ The first signs of 'Variegatum' are these dramatic new spring shoots.

*Prunus*

# cherry

**deciduous tree**

- *winter bark*
- *spring flowers*
- *fall foliage color*

*So much more than a mad spring flurry of blowsy flowers*

The spring burst of cherry flowers, whether in Britain's suburban gardens or on the Washington Mall, is just that: an almost overpowering spring outbreak of cliché, no sooner gasped at than it's over. Most of us are grateful that cherries are grown in someone else's garden; that way, we can admire them from afar, and we don't have to tolerate their dull and deadly boringness for fifty weeks of the year. But some cherries are different. A select few offer a two- to four-season contribution to the garden, on a modest scale and without clichéd effects, so that we can value them in our own situation rather than in other people's.

*Prunus cerasifera* 'Pissardii' and 'Nigra', the purple-leaved plums, have deep red unfurling spring foliage, purple foliage till fall, and a fine flurry of white ('Pissardii') or pink ('Nigra') flowers in spring.

*Prunus maackii* has reddish brown bark peeling like that of a birch tree, small white spring flowers carried in 2–3in/5–7.5cm dangling strings, black berries, and yellow fall color. 'Amber Beauty' is more erect, with lovely amber brown bark. 'Goldrush' ('Jeffree') has orange-brown to golden brown bark.

*Prunus sargentii* makes an elegant tree with spreading branches, the bark is chestnut brown, and the unfurling foliage is bronzed red. Then pink flowers open, creating an attractive rosy haze, followed by small black cherries. Then the fall color: spectacular in its fiery orange and scarlet tones, and the leaves turn before almost every other tree.

*Prunus serrula* has stunning bark: like a well-polished piece of old mahogany with additional cherrywood highlights, the bark gleams in winter and peels appealingly. The white flowers appear with the emerging leaves and are followed later by small red cherries.

▶ The pink flowers of 'Nigra' are followed by almost black foliage that lasts well into the fall.

## ESSENTIALS

- Site those with attractive bark where they can best be admired. Most are ideal shade trees with a light shadow, allowing many plants to be grown below.

- Happy in full sun in any reasonably fertile and well-drained soil that is not dry. Shelter from autumn winds will help prolong the fall color.

- Stake young trees securely until established. Prune in summer if necessary but little pruning is usually needed. Scrub the bark before winter to make the trunks gleam.

*Prunus cerasifera* 'Nigra'
Z5–9
30 × 30ft
9 × 9m

*Prunus cerasifera* 'Pissardii'
Z5–9
30 × 30ft
9 × 9m

*Prunus maackii*
Z3–7
30 × 25ft
9 × 8m

*Prunus maackii* 'Amber Beauty'
Z3–7
30 × 25ft
9 × 8m

*Prunus maackii* 'Goldrush' ('Jeffree')
Z3–7
30 × 25ft
9 × 8m

*Prunus sargentii*
Z5–9
70 × 50ft
21 × 15m

*Prunus serrula*
Z6–8
30 × 30ft
9 × 9m

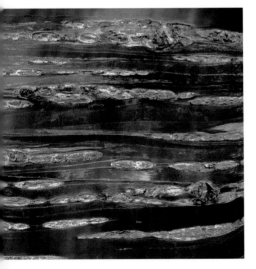

◀ The shining bark of *P. serrula*, an impressive all-year feature, is especially welcome in winter.

▲ The bark of *P. maackii* is perfect surrounded by *Cornus sanguinea* 'Winter Beauty'.

# lungwort

## *Pulmonaria*

**perennial**

You can hardly go wrong with pulmonarias. These beautiful, hardy, and resilient shade-loving perennials are amongst the most prized, but undeservedly neglected, of plants for their consistent reliability in producing sparkling spring flowers followed by prettily patterned spring and summer foliage, which lasts into autumn.

In a variety of both flower colors and leaf patterns, the plants are short, spread steadily, make good weed-suppressing ground cover, and are easy to propagate. The pretty little bell-shaped flowers may be white, red, various shades of pink, occasionally purple, but most often come in one of many shades of blue. As flowers age there can be many colors at once. The leaves emerge while the flowers are still open and vary in shape from long and narrow to broad and bold. Most are a dark, slightly bluish green enlivened by silver markings, which vary from a few scattered silver spots to more dense spotting; in some impressive cases, the leaves are almost entirely silvered. There are almost two hundred

different pulmonarias, but here are the best that embody our powerhouse theme.

'Cotton Cool' has pink buds opening to blue flowers in crowded clusters followed by long, narrow, rather upright leaves that are almost completely silver save for a slender green margin.

'David Ward', a selection of *P. rubra*, is one of the few variegated (as distinct from spotted) pulmonarias. Its pale green leaves with white edges are preceded by coral red flowers. Less robust than most, but impressive when thriving.

'Diana Clare' has large blue flowers with a purple stripe between each lobe, followed by long silver foliage with a green central vein and narrow green edge.

'Lewis Palmer' ('Highdown') is taller, with large dark purplish blue outward-facing flowers on upright stems followed by narrow dark green leaves boldly spotted in greenish white.

'Majesté' is one of the most widely grown of those with almost completely silver leaves; the unusually shiny foliage is

* *spring flowers*
* *spring to fall foliage*

*Some of the very best of powerhouse plants, almost all with three-season interest*

preceded by blue spring flowers opening from pink buds.

'Moonshine' has brilliantly silver mature summer foliage, with an uneven green edge itself slightly spotted. The palest blue spring flowers are small but generously produced. My favorite.

- Ideal as front-of-the-border specimens, pulmonarias associate well with other shade lovers, especially those with foliage in contrasting shapes and textures. Spring bulbs, too, make good neighbors, and the pulmonaria foliage will hide the dying bulb leaves.

- Best in partial or dappled shade, pulmonarias tolerate a variety of soil conditions though in dry conditions some may suffer from powdery mildew.

- Remove all the previous year's foliage before the new spring shoots emerge to allow the flowers to show themselves off effectively. Pulmonarias are easily lifted, split, and replanted elsewhere, but roots left behind may well resprout at the original location.

◀ While they appear together, the narrow, boldly spotted leaves of 'Lewis Palmer' ('Highdown') are the perfect background for the flower clusters.

▲ The almost completely silvery white foliage of 'Majesté' is enhanced by the green midrib and slender green edge.

*Pulmonaria* 'Cotton Cool'
  Z4–8
  8–12in
  20–30cm

*Pulmonaria* 'Diana Clare'
  Z4–8
  8–12in
  20–30cm

*Pulmonaria* 'Lewis Palmer'
  ('Highdown')
  Z5–8
  12–14in
  30–35cm

*Pulmonaria* 'Majesté'
  Z4–8
  8–12in
  20–30cm

*Pulmonaria* 'Moonshine'
  Z4–8
  8–12in
  20–30cm

*Pulmonaria rubra* 'David
  Ward'
  Z5–8
  10–12in
  25–30cm

▶ ▷ Most pulmonarias (here, 'Cotton Cool') tend to feature blue flowers opening from red or pink buds.

▷ ▶ The silvery leaves of 'Moonshine' are spectacular in high summer.

# rhododendron, azalea  *Rhododendron*

**evergreen or deciduous shrub**

We all know how spectacular rhododendrons can be in spring. Nothing quite compares with the overwhelming brilliance and vibrancy of their flowers. But that need not be their only display, for there is more to some of them than one spring knockout punch.

The new foliage of many rhododendrons brings an early surprise—often even the scales that enclose the new shoots can be attractive. As the leaves unroll and expand, they show off their color in two ways. Many have a dense hairy covering in silver or rusty shades on the undersides, and when the leaves first unfurl and are still in the vertical position this is the color that is revealed. Then as the foliage shifts steadily towards the horizontal and takes on its familiar flat shape, those with a similar colorful covering on the upper surface reveal it, if only briefly. This complexion on the upper surface then tends to fall away. Plants showing this intriguing feature include *R.*

*yakushimanum* and the many hybrids of this invaluable and hardy species, with clusters of flowers in a wide range of shades. But frankly, the best advice is to visit a rhododendron specialist in spring and assess the plants for the quality of their new foliage.

Later in the season, many varieties, especially of azaleas, develop spectacular fall color. Even evergreen azaleas lose their old foliage in the autumn, and the color can be amazingly fiery. Then, in winter, the leaves of some varieties, including the American favorite 'PJM', turn deep bronze purple in response to the cold before greening up again in spring.

Finally, a word about variegated rhododendrons. 'President Roosevelt', with an irregular yellow splash in the center of each leaf, was the old favorite, but its flowering can be erratic and it tends to flop. More are turning up now, including the more prolific and self-supporting 'Goldflimmer'.

- *spring flowers*
- *spring, fall, and winter foliage color*

*Fabulous color, not only from flowers but also with leaves, into autumn and winter*

*Rhododendron* 'Goldflimmer'
Z6–8
2–3 × 2–3ft
0.6–0.9 × 0.6–0.9m

*Rhododendron* 'Landmark'
Z5–9
3 × 4ft
0.9 × 1.2m

*Rhododendron* 'PJM'
Z4–8
4–6 × 4–6ft
1.2–1.8m × 1.2–1.8m

*Rhododendron* 'President Roosevelt'
Z7–9
4–6 × 4–6ft
1.2–1.8m × 1.2–1.8m

*Rhododendron yakushimanum*
Z5–9
2–3 × 2–3ft
0.6–0.9 × 0.6–0.9m

## ESSENTIALS

• *Rhododendron yakushimanum* and its hybrids are fine front-of-the-border specimens and also good container plants, while evergreen azaleas are good foundation plants and high ground cover.

• All require acid soil, preferably moist and rich in humus but not waterlogged. Many will take full sun, especially if conditions are not dry.

• Deadhead promptly after flowering, prune occasionally to maintain an elegant shape, and cut green shoots out from variegated forms.

◀ When 'Landmark' loses its oldest leaves in autumn, their vibrant coloring is amazing and, in fact, rather similar to the coloring of its spring flowers. Winter leaves are bronze.

▲ In winter the foliage of many evergreen rhododendrons, including 'PJM', turns this lovely purplish bronze.

▲ The downy coating on the leaves of *R. yakushimanum* dusts off of the upper surface but remains on the lower.

*Rosa*

# rose

**deciduous shrub or vine**

- *spring shoots*
- *fragrant spring or summer flowers*
- *fall foliage color and fruits*

*Foliage and fruits add to the familiar charm of prolific flowers*

Roses are amongst the most beloved of all flowers, and with fragrance as well as color, most are easily powerhouse plants. But here I have in mind two other features to add: foliage color (both new bronzed shoots and fall color) and especially the fruits—rose hips. Of course, the gardener's natural tendency to deadhead roses must be restrained, otherwise there will be no hips at all!

▶ ▷ The large and fragrant flowers of *R. rugosa* open from June intermittently all summer and towards the end of the season will sit alongside the maturing hips.

▷ ▶ 'Fru Dagmar Hastrup' has pretty, slightly puckered foliage, clove-scented flowers, and deep red hips.

## ESSENTIALS

- Roses come in a wide array of shapes, sizes, and growing styles, so be sure to give ground-cover types and ramblers the space they need and allow bushier types to develop into mature specimens. Most are enhanced by planting clematis vines to scramble though them, matching the color and vigor of the clematis to its host.

- Most roses enjoy full sun and any good fertile soil that is neither waterlogged nor often dry.

- Pruning is essential for most, but different roses need different styles of pruning to bring out their best qualities. Only ramblers guided into trees can be allowed unfettered freedom.

▶ 'Wild Thing' ('Jactoose') has large, single pink flowers and orange-red, pear-shaped hips that are especially good for jam and tea.

Most roses produce colorful hips, but in many they are small or otherwise unexceptional, and the crop may be unpredictable. Those roses that consistently produce good hips after a colorful display of flowers fall into four groups: old heirloom shrub roses, modern shrub roses, rambling roses, and wild species and their near relatives, including the British *R. canina* and the North American *R.*

*virginiana*. These native wild roses (and indeed most of my recommended choices) have single flowers, which may be less long-lasting than doubles but which often produce hips more reliably.

*Rosa glauca* has grayish leaves with purple tints, pink single flowers, bright red hips, yellow fall color—and is almost thornless. For best summer leaf color, site in a little shade.

*Rosa macrophylla* has clear pink single flowers, followed by large, flagon-shaped orange hips, which in 'Master Hugh' are especially huge.

*Rosa moyesii* is widely grown for its dependably produced orange-red hips, which follow the deep red single flowers. 'Geranium', with orange-red flowers, is more modest in growth.

*Rosa pimpinellifolia* is unusually spiny, but its creamy flowers are followed by jet black hips. Good in poor soils.

*Rosa rugosa* and its hybrids are perhaps the best in combining large and colorful flowers with large and reliable hips. 'Fru Dagmar Hastrup' has clear pink flowers followed by rich crimson hips; 'Scabrosa' has huge crimson flowers and enormous orange-red hips. Avoid the popular 'Roseraie de l'Hay', which sets no hips at all.

Of the old heirloom shrub roses, my choices are three. 'Buff Beauty' is a lovely arching Hybrid Musk with bronzed young leaves, a long season of superbly fragrant rich apricot yellow flowers, and orange hips. 'Lady Penzance' is a dense growing and vigorous Sweet Briar (Eglantine) with golden-centered pink flowers, aromatic foliage, and bright red hips. 'Maxima' is a tall Alba rose for the back of the border with fragrant, blowsy double white flowers, grayish foliage, and orange hips.

Some modern shrub roses, developed with disease resistance and a long flowering season in mind, also feature good hips to follow those abundant flowers. In 'Bonica' ('Meidomonac') the slightly scented pink flowers and spherical red hips are carried on a spreading, ground-covering plant. 'Nymphenburg' is a gangly, back-of-the-border shrub with apple-scented salmon pink flowers followed by red hips. 'Wild Thing' ('Jactoose'), an unusually healthy rose with an arching and informal, almost wild style, has lightly scented

◄ The fresh new foliage of 'Wild Thing' ('Jactoose') is attractive even before the carmine buds appear.

▲ 'Bonica' ('Meidomonac'), one of the best of recent roses, offers these very double flowers and, later, hips in abundance.

▶ 'Nymphenburg', another modern shrub rose, may be counted on for abundant red hips.

dark pink flowers and orange-red hips.

Finally, many rambling roses produce hips, often small but in very large clusters, which last well into winter. These are all vigorous plants, often best trained up into a tree. 'Frances E. Lester' features large open sprays of fragrant white flowers with pink tints at the edges followed by small red hips, all set against slightly coppery foliage. 'Kiftsgate', a selection of *R. filipes*, is a well-known classic with fragrant, creamy white flowers in clusters of over a hundred followed by red hips; it's slow to start, but worth the wait. 'Rambling Rector' has semi-double flowers with well-scented, cupped white flowers followed by orange hips.

*Rosa* 'Bonica' ('Meidomonac')
Z4–9
3 × 6ft
0.9 × 1.8m

*Rosa* 'Buff Beauty'
Z6–9
5 × 5ft
1.5 × 1.5m

*Rosa canina*
Z3–9
10 × 8ft
3 × 2.4m

*Rosa filipes* 'Kiftsgate'
Z6–9
25 × 25ft
8 × 8m

*Rosa* 'Frances E. Lester'
Z5–9
15 × 10ft
4.5 × 3m

*Rosa* 'Fru Dagmar Hastrup'
Z2–9
7 × 6ft
2.1 × 1.8m

*Rosa glauca*
Z2–8
6 × 5ft
1.8 × 1.5m

*Rosa* 'Lady Penzance'
Z3–9
7 × 6ft
2.1 × 1.8m

*Rosa macrophylla*
Z5–9
10 × 4ft
3 × 1.2m

*Rosa macrophylla* 'Master Hugh'
Z5–9
10 × 4ft
3 × 1.2m

*Rosa* 'Maxima'
Z3–9
6 × 4ft
1.8 × 1.2m

*Rosa moyesii*
Z5–9
10 × 4ft
3 × 1.2m

*Rosa moyesii* 'Geranium'
Z5–9
10 × 4ft
3 × 1.2m

*Rosa* 'Nymphenburg'
Z4–9
6 × 4ft
1.8 × 1.2m

*Rosa pimpinellifolia*
Z3–9
3 × 3ft
90 × 90cm

*Rosa* 'Rambling Rector'
Z5–9
20 × 15ft
6 × 4.5m

*Rosa rugosa*
Z2–9
7 × 6ft
2.1 × 1.8m

*Rosa* 'Scabrosa'
Z2–9
7 × 6ft
2.1 × 1.8m

*Rosa virginiana*
Z3–9
4 × 5ft
1.2 × 1.5m

*Rosa* 'Wild Thing' ('Jactoose')
Z5–9
3 × 4ft
0.9 × 1.2m

## Rubus

# bramble, blackberry, raspberry

**deciduous shrub**

- *winter stems*
- *summer foliage*
- *fall fruits*

*Tough and dependable, with bright winter stems and more color later in the season*

A few brambles are justifiably well known for their winter stem whiteness, the bright waxy coating that almost gleams even on dull winter days. But for most of them, *R. bicolor*, *R. cockburnianus* —what next? Their foliage is perfectly nice but not outstanding. Their flowers come in white clusters but are not especially impressive. Their fruits are small and appealing to small creatures and birds (the latter at least are good to have around) but do not boast much bright ornamental appeal. So . . . where does that leave us? It leaves us with *R. cockburnianus* 'Goldenvale' and with black raspberries.

'Goldenvale' is a very

▶ ▷ With these two distinct looks, winter and summer, 'Goldenvale' is a most striking plant and valuable in most gardens.

▷ ▶ In winter, the pink stems of black raspberries stand out against the snow.

- Blue-flowered plants make ideal partners, so plan for a succession, from blue scilla or chionodoxa amongst those white stems in early spring to blue columbines in front in early summer. Later, the summer growth of brambles makes a stout support for 'Heavenly Blue' morning glory. Three seasons of color combinations.

- Happy in any soil that does not dry out, in sun or partial shade.

- For stems, cut back hard in early spring, as the scillas fade, and strong new growth will soon develop. For fruit, cut out old shoots after harvest.

▶ The fruits of black raspberries are both attractive and tasty, and the summer stems have a silvery look.

valuable plant. There are no flamboyant flowers, and the fruits are not exactly outstanding. But after its bright interlacing network of white winter stems, the foliage emerges—in bright yellow. Not only that, but 'Goldenvale' is less vigorous: it spreads less strongly than its green-leaved progenitor so is welcome in small gardens as well as large. Its small flowers are rosy purple, its fall fruits are black. But the long season of yellow foliage is invaluable, especially on such a tough plant.

And then there are those black raspberries . . . Derived from the white-stemmed American native *R. occidenta-*

*lis*, the berries mature to jet black in midsummer and boast a distinctive not-quite-raspberry, not-quite-blackberry flavor. Be sure to get to them before the birds and small quadrupeds do. 'Haut' is prolific and matures over a long season; 'Jewel' is especially easy to pick and disease resistant; 'Munger' is sweet, disease resistant, and with relatively few seeds.

Then in winter, like 'Goldenvale', the white stems gleam on through, often revealing their underlying pinkish red coloring. Stouter, and less twiggy than the stems of 'Goldenvale', they arch elegantly and gleam with ice on winter mornings.

*Rubus cockburnianus*
  **'Goldenvale'**
  Z5–9
  5 × 8ft
  1.5 × 2.4m

*Rubus occidentalis* **'Haut'**
  Z5–9
  3 × 6ft
  0.9 × 1.8m untrained

*Rubus occidentalis* **'Jewel'**
  Z5–9
  3 × 6ft
  0.9 × 1.8m untrained

*Rubus occidentalis* **'Munger'**
  Z5–9
  3 × 6ft
  0.9 × 1.8m untrained

# Asian hydrangea vine    *Schizophragma*

**deciduous vine**

*Schizophragma hydrangeoides* is a self-clinging climbing member of the hydrangea family native to Japan. Its white lacecap flowerheads, up to 10in/25cm across and impressive both in their size and the purity of their white coloring, gleam against dense foliage in summer.

And those leaves. In the

- *winter stems*
- *spring to fall foliage*
- *summer flowers*
- *fall foliage color*

*A long season of foliar attractions, with large lacecap flowers in summer*

◀ The prettily patterned foliage of 'Moonlight' is attractive for many months, and in summer these broad white lacecaps open.

variety 'Moonlight', held on reddish stalks and appealingly heart-shaped, the reddish coloring seeps into the leaf's midrib, which then breaks into a neat green network of veins, between which the silvery patina shines. The foliage is a little reminiscent of a silvery heuchera and may even develop a red rim. In summer, the broad lacecap heads feature an irregular ring of almost heart-shaped white sepals around a cluster of small white florets, all held on pale reddish orange stalks. Come the fall, the leaves all turn buttery yellow, and the red coloring in their stalks becomes more vivid. The flowers change to warm brown tones, similar to shrubby

hydrangeas. After leaf fall, the emerging winter stems feature; they too are well colored, a bright pinkish red.

'Moonlight' is exceptional, but the green-leaved species is itself a fine plant with its white summer flowerheads and yellow fall color; there is even a pretty rose pink flowered form, 'Roseum'.

Larger in all its parts, and often more spectacular in flower than 'Moonlight' but without the stylish foliage, is *S. integrifolium*. Its white flowerheads can be 12in/30cm across, and each white sepal may be 3in/7.5cm long—so the effect is impressive. The green, smooth-edged leaves make a fine background and turn yellow in fall.

*Schizophragma hydrangeoides*
  Z6–9
  30–40 × 5–15ft
  9–12 × 1.5–4.5m

*Schizophragma hydrangeoides*
  **'Moonlight'**
  Z6–9
  30–40 × 5–15ft
  9–12 × 1.5–4.5m

*Schizophragma hydrangeoides*
  **'Roseum'**
  Z6–9
  30–40 × 5–15ft
  9–12 × 1.5–4.5m

*Schizophragma integrifolium*
  Z6–9
  30–40 × 5–15ft
  9–12 × 1.5–4.5m

## ESSENTIALS

- Best trained to climb a tree trunk and left to show itself off uncluttered. Large hostas or smaller to medium rhododendrons can be planted near the base to hide what may sometimes be bare basal stems.

- Make a good planting site at the base of a tree by digging as large a hole as possible between the tree's roots and adding a fertile soil mix. Can be grown on a north wall but flowers better in more light. Dislikes very limey soil. Slow to settle after planting, but determined.

- After planting, tape shoots to the tree trunk to encourage them to climb. No pruning needed unless the plant becomes too large.

◀ In fall, the bright yellowing leaf color of 'Moonlight' is sparked by the red leaf stalks in one final fling of the season.

## Sorbus

# mountainash

**deciduous tree**

- *fragrant spring flowers*
- *summer foliage*
- *fall foliage color and fruits*

*Essential three-season trees for gardens large and small*

These are classic powerhouse plants—in fact, mountain-ash brings us *three* distinct features (two with shifting characters) from one attractive tree. First, in spring, the flowers: flat or slightly domed heads of white fluffy florets line the branches, set prettily against the newly opened, rich dark green leaves, neatly divided into opposite pairs of leaflets, for a beautifully symmetric look. During the summer, the foliage is the main feature, clothing an elegant tree which is ideal as the only specimen in a small yard. Finally, the berries, which begin to ripen during the

▶ ▷ The dusty cream flower-heads of *S. americana* are followed by clusters of bright berries, all set against handsome divided foliage which turns orange in fall.

▷ ▶ The British native *S. aucuparia* produces dense clusters of colorful berries.

of variation, in particular in the summer leaf color, the richness of the flower color, and especially in the habit of the plants. The color of the stems can also be significant, orange or reddish stems sometimes being more striking than green. Your choice may be partly governed by what happens to be available at your favorite nursery, and there is also the undeniable fact that some gardeners (especially men, it seems) cannot take the combination of bright pink flowers set against bright yellow foliage: they simply will not grow these plants at all.

'Candlelight' has bright butter yellow spring leaves maturing to gold then greening a little before turning fiery red in fall. The flowers are purplish pink.

'Double Play Big Bang' ('Tracy') has orange spring foliage becoming yellow then greeny yellow later, so the very large pink flowers are set against foliage in a relatively soft shade.

'Golden Princess' ('Lisp') is reddish bronze in spring maturing to bright gold then increasingly orange in fall. The flowers are purplish pink.

'Goldflame' was the first of the bright yellow types and remains popular. Rich orange-red in spring, then yellowish green, and orange in fall with deep pink flowers. May produce green shoots and get mildew.

'Magic Carpet' ('Walbuma') is low and mounded, especially at first, with bright red new shoots maturing through yellowish green to fiery fall tones, with purplish pink flowers.

## ESSENTIALS

- Effective in spring with daffodils in yellow and orange combinations, and with dark-leaved elderberries behind to help show their colors.

- Happy in most soils that are not waterlogged or parched. Most enjoy full sun but if scorched in summer, a little shade will help. Scorching happens most often when plants are dry.

- Nip off the fading flowerheads, leaving the foliage to develop fall color. For the best foliage color, or to renovate, cut back very hard in spring.

◀ 'Goldflame' brings a love-it-or-hate-it combination of yellow foliage and pink flowers.

*Spiraea* **'Candlelight'**
Z4–9
20–30 × 36–40in
50–75 × 90–100cm

*Spiraea* **'Double Play Big Bang'** ('Tracy')
Z4–9
24–36 × 28–40in
60–90 × 70–100cm

*Spiraea* **'Golden Princess'** ('Lisp')
Z4–9
24–30 × 24–30in
60–75 × 60–75cm

*Spiraea* **'Goldflame'**
Z4–9
26–40 × 36–40in
65–100 × 90–100cm

*Spiraea* **'Magic Carpet'** ('Walbuma')
Z3–9
28–36 × 36–40in
70–90 × 90–100cm

# celandine poppy

**biennial or short-lived perennial**

- *early spring rosette*
- *late spring flowers*
- *summer seedpods*

*Unique foliage gives way to sparkling flowers on politely self-seeding plants*

Considering their long season of changing appeal, their tolerant nature, the ease with which they can be grown in a variety of situations, and their propensity to seed themselves around just enough, we really should come across these plants more often. An American and an Asian species are our choices. The American *S. diphyllum* is rather like a supercharged version of the European greater celandine (*Chelidonium majus*), which is now settling in over much of the American continent. From attractive rosettes of bluish green, oak-leaved foliage (evergreen in milder areas), upright stems carry four-petaled golden flowers in spring. It grows wild through the East and makes a fine garden companion to Virginia bluebells (*Mertensia virginica*)

and bloodroot (*Sanguinaria canadensis*).

The pick, however, is the Asian *S. lasiocarpum*, which by its first autumn has developed appealing, rather tightly formed, soft pale leafy rosettes of very distinctive foliage: split into a few opposite pairs of jagged edged leaflets with one much larger leaflet at the tip. The leaves are gently downy underneath, and the whole of this slightly brittle plant is filled with reddish orange sap. Then, in spring, smartly upright shoots carry bright, four-petalled yellow poppy flowers; each flower is relatively short-lived, but they open over a long period. Finally, in summer, the very slender pods develop and stretch to about 3in/7.5cm in length.

▶ The leaves of *S. lasiocarpum* are unusual for their large segment at the tip, soft texture, and slightly yellowish color cast.

*Stylophorum diphyllum*
Z4–8
20 × 30in
50 × 75cm

*Stylophorum lasiocarpum*
Z4–8
18 × 18in
45 × 45cm

elevated them from "simply pretty but unremarkable" to essential shade perennials.

'Mystic Mist' tops the list. In spring, the soft, neatly lobed, more or less triangular foliage is bright green, evenly speckled with white. Spikes of white flowers are held on red stems in late spring, and by early summer the main leaf veins are recast in crimson. As fall approaches, pinkish leaf tinges start to take over,

- Ideal as part of the shade garden tapestry, continuing interest through summer and autumn and into winter, a time when many good partners, including primroses, hellebores, and anemones, are past their best. Running types will fill shady spaces under shrubs, while clump-forming types make intriguing small specimens.

- Clump-forming tiarellas enjoy shade, moisture, and good drainage; running types are happy with less moisture.

- Nipping the flower stalks off as they fade improves the look of the plants immeasurably. Clump formers can be split every three or four years, but replant fairly closely to give the illusion of one large clump. Weevil grubs may munch through the crowns; biological control is effective.

◀ Fresh new foliage and a mass of pink-tipped flower spikes on 'Sugar and Spice'.

▲ The flowers have faded on 'Sugar and Spice', by which time the green leaves are boldly marked in almost black.

be a long and slightly cumbersome name, but there is universal agreement that the doublefile viburnum, as it is sometimes known, is amongst the finest of flowering shrubs. Its unique tiered growth—the branches are held in a series of almost parallel horizontal layers—is less clearly defined in winter, but as soon as the new shoots begin to emerge in spring, the structure becomes evident. The foliage is rich green, attractively pleated, so much so that the veins catch the light. In late spring and early summer, the white lacecap flowerheads line the upper sides of the branches, laid out alternately in two rows, creating a huge white lacy confection. The flowers give way to red fruits, which eventually turn black (if the birds allow), and the slightly pale wine red fall color that follows is sparked by brighter or pinker tones. This is a stupendous plant and, as I have recently discovered, a mature specimen happily takes to being moved and cut back ferociously if it outgrows its space. Dislikes drought, though.

In the somewhat undignified scramble for the runners-up spots, seven other species stand out.

*Viburnum acerifolium.* One of the most resilient species, with 2–3in/5–7.5cm clusters of just off-white flowers followed

- Most viburnums fruit more prolifically if more than one form of the same species is planted in the same garden. Surround with bulbs and shorter perennials (medium-sized hostas, epimediums, pulmonarias).

- Most are unfussy, enjoying full sun or partial shade in any reasonable soil. Other preferences are noted.

- Little pruning is generally needed, except perhaps to improve their shape. Old and woody plants can be rejuvenated by cutting back hard.

◀ ◁ *Viburnum carlesii* brings particularly bright fall color to the shrub border.

◁ ◀ The white summer flowers (and eventually blue berries) of 'Blue Muffin' ('Christom') are carried on a compact "muffin" of a plant.

by red berries that quickly turn purplish black and last into winter. In between, lovely maple-like foliage is rosy then develops burgundy tones over a long fall season. A North American native, happy in dry soil and deep shade.

*Viburnum carlesii*. An unbeatable combination of red flower buds and white flowers in the same rounded spring cluster, exquisite fragrance, and wine red fall color—but inconsistent berries. Look for 'Aurora', 'Charis', and 'Diana', which last also has purplish new shoots.

*Viburnum dentatum*. Robust and adaptable North American native opening its white flowers in late spring and ripening its dark bluish fruits around the same time as its yellow or red autumn color. 'Blue Muffin' ('Christom') is compact and with especially blue berries.

*Viburnum dilatatum*. Another fine flower–fruit– fall foliage combination from another North American native. The white flowerheads (unpleasantly scented, sadly) are up to 5in/12.5cm across, and the berries ripen to bright

red and last into winter, while the fall foliage color tends to russet or purplish tones, often in combination with those long-lasting berries.

*Viburnum opulus.* The most impressive plant amongst the European native viburnums and enjoys most conditions. White lacecap flowers open in early summer, followed later by long-lasting glistening red berries and dark reddish or purplish autumn color. The neat 'Compactum' flowers and fruits freely, while the slow 'Aureum' is shorter with yellow foliage. 'Xanthocarpum' has yellow fruits, and the less elegant 'Roseum' has faintly pink-tinted flowers in rounded heads like a mophead or big-leaf hydrangea.

*Viburnum tinus.* The only evergreen of my viburnum choices with dark foliage, white winter flowers, and blue-black fruits. 'Gwenllian' has deep pink flower buds and fruits reliably; 'Eve Price' is slow with carmine buds and pale pink flowers. But look out for two variegated forms, 'Variegatum' and the uncommon but brighter 'Bewley's Variegated'.

*Viburnum trilobum.* The North American version of the European *V. opulus* differs in small botanical features but is also hardier and more dependable in American gardens.

White, early summer lacecap flowers, bright red berries that mature from yellow, and red fall color provide three features; and several, including 'Hans' and 'Wentworth', have been selected for their edible fruits.

New viburnums appear regularly, and all are worth checking for their multiple features.

◀ Between the flowers and the fall foliage of 'Mariesii', the red fruits turn black and are eaten by birds.

▶ The bright red, late-ripening fruits of 'Wentworth' are edible.

*Viburnum acerifolium*
Z4–8
3 × 4ft
0.9 × 1.2m

*Viburnum carlesii* 'Aurora'
Z5–8
6 × 6ft
1.8 × 1.8m

*Viburnum carlesii* 'Charis'
Z5–8
6 × 6ft
1.8 × 1.8m

*Viburnum carlesii* 'Diana'
Z5–8
6 × 6ft
1.8 × 1.8m

*Viburnum dentatum*
Z3–8
10 × 10ft
3 × 3m

*Viburnum dentatum* 'Blue Muffin' ('Christom')
Z3–8
10 × 10ft
3 × 3m

*Viburnum dilatatum*
Z5–8
10 × 6ft
3 × 1.8m

*Viburnum opulus*
Z4–8
15 × 12ft
4.5 × 3.5m

*Viburnum opulus* 'Aureum'
Z4–8
12 × 10ft
3.5 × 3m

*Viburnum opulus* 'Compactum'
Z4–8
5 × 5ft
1.5 × 1.5m

*Viburnum opulus* 'Roseum'
Z4–8
15 × 12ft
4.5 × 3.5m

*Viburnum opulus* 'Xanthocarpum'
Z4–8
15 × 12ft
4.5 × 3.5m

*Viburnum plicatum* f. *tomentosum* 'Mariesii'
Z4–8
10 × 12ft
3 × 3.5m

*Viburnum tinus*
Z6–8
10 × 10ft
3 × 3m

*Viburnum tinus* 'Bewley's Variegated'
Z6–8
8 × 5ft
2.4 × 1.5m

*Viburnum tinus* 'Eve Price'
Z6–8
8 × 5ft
2.4 × 1.5m

*Viburnum tinus* 'Gwenllian'
Z6–8
10 × 10ft
3 × 3m

*Viburnum tinus* 'Variegatum'
Z6–8
8 × 5ft
2.4 × 1.5m

*Viburnum trilobum*
Z2–7
15 × 12ft
4.5 × 3.5m

*Viburnum trilobum* 'Hans'
Z2–7
15 × 12ft
4.5 × 3.5m

*Viburnum trilobum* 'Wentworth'
Z2–7
15 × 12ft
4.5 × 3.5m

# weigela

**deciduous shrub**

Gardeners have been very fortunate in recent years. From a choice of just one dark-leaved and one variegated weigela that we enjoyed for so long, we now have around a dozen of each. From first opening, they bring us foliage either in bronze or purplish or wine red shades, or edged in white, cream, or yellow, then burst into flowers ranging from deep red through to white. This increasing range

• *spring to fall foliage*

• *spring or summer flowers*

*Three seasons of lively or sultry foliage, vividly transformed by late spring flowers*

◀ In late spring and early summer, the yellow variegation, red buds, and pink flowers of 'French Lace' ('Brigela', 'Moulin Rouge') are stunning; later, the shrub's effect is much more subtle.

of attractive choices is especially valuable in a plant so easy to grow, for weigelas are very hardy—resilient in less than ideal conditions and robust in the face of neglect. The old shrubberies of the past were known for their unkillable evergreens, but weigelas often survived amongst them. I should warn that in modern weigelas, the names can be confusing, and the same plant may be sold under more than one name.

Dark-leaved varieties provide solidity and anchorage in mixed borders. Attractive in their own right, and with flowers that harmonize beautifully with the leaves, they can also be the focal point for planting combinations in a wide range of complementary and contrasting colors, textures, and shapes. 'Black and White' ('Courtacad1') is the most dramatic of these. Dwarf and widely spreading, the deep plummy foliage turns almost black by midsummer and sets off the white flowers clearly.

'Fine Wine' ('Bramwell') is also dwarf and spreading, but with richer foliage and pink flowers. 'Midnight Wine' ('Elvera') is similar but even more dwarf, though a little less hardy. 'Minor Black' ('Verweig3') is between 'Fine

Wine' and 'Midnight Wine' in size, with dark reddish brown leaves and purplish pink flowers.

'Naomi Campbell' ('Bokrashine', 'Shining Sensation') has polished burgundy foliage, a superb partner for its pink flowers, and although the flowers come in a furious flurry in May and June, they continue sporadically all summer.

'Spilled Wine' ('Bokraspiwi') is the color of my evening tipple (assuming I bought the good stuff), and its slightly wavy foliage adds to the appeal. The magenta pink flowers make appropriate bright companions, but 'Spilled Wine' is also worth treating as a foliage plant, cutting back hard in spring and missing the flowers.

'Wine and Roses' ('Alexandra') is now the most widely grown purple-leaved variety, larger than many, so with more impact. Vivid pink flowers look good with the purplish bronze leaves, which soften in tone by midsummer.

Sometimes less vigorous and less tough, variegated forms nevertheless provide impressive long-season foliage color. And, in late spring, their second feature takes over as they become emblazoned

**ESSENTIALS**

- Larger types are impressive as anchors in mixed borders or as mid border specimens. Smaller varieties, besides thriving in containers, are good as frontal focal points or overhanging the edge of raised beds.

- Happy in any reasonable soil; most enjoy full sun yet also thrive in a little shade. Variegated varieties may scorch in full sun, especially in dry spells. In containers, drying out is always an issue, but drip irrigation will help solve that problem. Pests and diseases are rare.

- Pruning is the only regular care weigelas need. When the first flowers have faded, cut out all the shoots lined with developing seedpods to promote new growth to flower the following year.

◀ In early summer 'Wine and Roses' ('Alexandra') is at its peak, a powerful combination of rich dark foliage and cerise pink flowers.

with contrasting red flowers, or with pink flowers in a more harmonious shade.

'Florida Variegata', for many decades the most widely grown (and lone) variegated form, remains an excellent plant, its relatively narrow leaves edged in cream, often sporting pinkish tints. The flowers, in pink shades, can almost completely mask the leaves, but the two colors work well together when juxtaposed.

'French Lace' ('Brigela', 'Moulin Rouge') provides the best contrast between rich red flowers and yellow-edged green leaves.

'Magical Rainbow' ('Kolmagira', 'Rainbow Sensation') features broad foliage with yellow margins and strong red tints, especially in the young growth. The variegation does not fade or scorch but contrasts well with the unexpectedly red stems and the pink flowers.

*Weigela* 'Black and White' ('Courtacad1')
Z5–8
12–24 × 24–30in
30–60 × 60–75cm

*Weigela florida* 'Fine Wine' ('Bramwell')
Z4–8
2–3 × 2–3ft
0.6–0.9 × 0.6–0.9m

*Weigela florida* 'French Lace' ('Brigela', 'Moulin Rouge')
Z4–8
6 × 4ft
1.8 × 1.2m

*Weigela florida* 'Magical Rainbow' ('Kolmagira', 'Rainbow Sensation')
Z5–8
4 × 4ft
1.2 × 1.2m

*Weigela florida* 'Midnight Wine' ('Elvera')
Z5–8
10–12 × 10–12in
25–30 × 25–30cm

*Weigela florida* 'Minor Black' ('Verweig3')
Z5–8
24–30 × 24–30in
60–75 × 60–75cm

*Weigela florida* 'Spilled Wine' ('Bokraspiwi')
Z4–8
2 × 3ft
0.6 × 0.9m

*Weigela* 'Florida Variegata'
Z5–8
5 × 5ft
1.5 × 1.5m

*Weigela florida* 'Wine and Roses' ('Alexandra')
Z4–8
4 × 4ft
1.2 × 1.2m

*Weigela* 'Naomi Campbell' ('Bokrashine', 'Shining Sensation')
Z5–8
5 × 4ft
1.5 × 1.2m

▶ The foliage color of 'Wine and Roses' ('Alexandra') is at its richest when plants are grown in full sun.

# Nursery Sources

Powerhouse plants can be found in the garden departments of big box stores and DIY stores, but local nurseries often provide the best advice and are usually better able to guide your choices. If you see an attractive plant on sale, anywhere, remember the mantra: "What else does it do?"

In many cases, choosing plants with multiple seasons of interest is all about selecting exactly the right variety—not all hostas have colorful fall foliage. When local outlets don't carry the right variety, turn to mail order sources.

## UK and Ireland

Bluebell Arboretum and
  Nursery
bluebellnursery.com

Bressingham Gardens
bressinghamgardens.com

Burncoose Nurseries
burncoose.co.uk

Cally Gardens
callygardens.co.uk

Camolin Potting Shed
camolinpottingshed.com

Chiltern Seeds
chilternseeds.co.uk

Claire Austin Hardy Plants
claireaustin-hardyplants.co.uk

Cotswold Garden Flowers
cgf.net

Crocus
crocus.co.uk

Crûg Farm
crug-farm.co.uk

Farmyard Nurseries
farmyardnurseries.co.uk

Fernatix
fernatix.co.uk

Great Dixter Nurseries
greatdixter.co.uk/nursery.htm

Hardy's Cottage Garden Plants
hardys-plants.co.uk

Harveys Garden Plants
harveysgardenplants.co.uk

Hayloft Plants
hayloft-plants.co.uk

Heucheraholics
heucheraholics.co.uk

Hillier Garden Centres
hillieronline.co.uk

Hoecroft Plants
hoecroft.co.uk

Hopleys Plants
hopleys.co.uk

Knoll Gardens
knollgardens.co.uk

Long Acre Plants
plantsforshade.co.uk

Madrona Nursery
madrona.co.uk

Margery Fish Plant Nursery
eastlambrook.co.uk

Park Green Nurseries
parkgreen.co.uk

Peter Beales Roses
classicroses.co.uk

Plantagogo
plantagogo.com

Simply Seeds and Plants
simplyseedsandplants.co.uk

Special Plants
specialplants.net

Stillingfleet Lodge
stillingfleetlodgenurseries.co.uk

Thorncroft Clematis
thorncroftclematis.co.uk

Winchester Growers
national-dahlia-collection.
co.uk

## North America

American Beauties
abnativeplants.com

Arrowhead Alpines
arrowhead-alpines.com

Baker Creek Heirloom Seeds
rareseeds.com

Bluestem Nursery
bluestem.ca

Bluestone Perennials
bluestoneperennials.com

Brent and Becky's Bulbs
brentandbeckysbulbs.com

Brushwood Nursery
gardenvines.com

Collector's Nursery
collectorsnursery.com

Digging Dog Nursery
diggingdog.com

Edelweiss Perennials
edelweissperennials.com

Evermay Nursery
evermaynursery.com

Fancy Fronds
fancyfronds.com

Forest Farm
forestfarm.com

Garden Crossings
gardencrossings.com

Garden Vision
home.earthlink.net/~ darrellpro

Great Garden Plants
greatgardenplants.com

Greenwood Nursery
greenwoodnursery.com

Heirloom Roses
heirloomroses.com

Heronswood
heronswood.com

High Country Gardens
highcountrygardens.com

Hostas Direct
hostasdirect.com

Joy Creek Nursery
joycreek.com

Klehm's Song Sparrow
songsparrow.com

Nature Hills Nursery
naturehills.com

Niche Gardens
nichegardens.com

North Creek Nurseries
northcreeknurseries.com

Plant Delights
plantdelights.com

Rare Find
rarefindnursery.com

Romence
romencegardens.com

Wayside
waysidegardens.com

White Flower Farm
whiteflowerfarm.com

# Index

Photograph pages 2–3: Bright winter and early spring dogwood stems shine against a background of purple and white hybrid crocuses, with some in yellow reflecting the color in the stems.

Photograph pages 26–27: Three plants create an exciting combination. *Phlox paniculata* 'Goldmine' provides vivid cerise flowers and variegated foliage, *Eryngium planum* 'Blaukappe' brings us prettily patterned early leaves and blue summer flowers. In the background, the striped foliage of *Miscanthus sinensis* 'Variegatus' will be followed by reddish plumes.

Copyright © 2013 by Graham Rice. All rights reserved.

Photo on page 48 by Kathi Rogers; photo on page 67 by Tim Fross. All other photography © judywhite and Graham Rice GardenPhotos.com.

Published in 2013 by Timber Press, Inc.

The Haseltine Building
133 S.W. Second Avenue, Suite 450
Portland, Oregon 97204-3527
timberpress.com

2 The Quadrant
135 Salusbury Road
London NW6 6RJ
timberpress.co.uk

Printed in China
Book design by Susan Applegate

Library of Congress Cataloging-in-Publication Data

Rice, Graham.
  Powerhouse plants: 510 top performers for multi-season beauty/ Graham Rice; photography by judywhite and Graham Rice.—1st ed.
      p. cm.
  Includes index.
  ISBN 978-1-60469-210-5 (alk. paper)
  1. Landscape gardening. 2. Plants, Ornamental. I. White, Judy. II. Title.
  SB453.R524 2013
  635.9—dc23                                    2012010486

A catalog record for this book is also available from the British Library.

**GRAHAM RICE** is a distinguished international garden writer and is unique in having won three awards for his writing in the USA—and also three in the UK. He is editor-in-chief of the *American Horticultural Society's Encyclopedia of Perennials* and the author of more than twenty books, and he runs the Royal Horticultural Society's New Plants blog as well as his Transatlantic Gardener blog. He has been the gardening correspondent of Britain's *Observer* and *Evening Standard* newspapers and contributes frequently to the RHS's magazines *The Garden* and *The Plantsman*; he has also written for all the top gardening magazines on both sides of the Atlantic, including *Horticulture, Garden Design, BBC Gardeners' World*, and *Country Life*. A widely respected plantsman, Graham trained at the prestigious Royal Botanic Gardens, Kew, is a member of the RHS's Herbaceous Plants Committee (judging their trials of both annuals and perennials), and also judges at the Chelsea Flower Show. He is married to author and photographer judywhite; they live and garden in Milford, Pennsylvania, and in Northamptonshire, UK.